RADIO
PROGRAMMING
AND BRANDING

THE ULTIMATE PODCASTING AND RADIO BRANDING GUIDE

GARY BEGIN

Published by:
Library Tales Publishing, Inc.
511 6th Avenue #56
New York, NY 10011
www.LibraryTalesPublishing.com

ISBN-13: 978-0692331491
ISBN-10: 0692331492

PRINTED IN THE UNITED STATES OF AMERICA

TABLE OF CONTENTS

FOREWORD

In the midst of several decades, radio broadcasting has had to endure many turning points. There was the creation of networks in the '20s and '30s, including NBC, CBS, and Mutual, and in the 1940s there was ABC. Radio became a main source of information and entertainment both locally and on the major networks. During the depression and World War II, President Roosevelt calmed the country with his fireside chats.

Radio was a major part of the American fabric. Many small station licenses, mostly AM, were issued by the FCC after the war. Radio's first major challenge came from the launch of television in the late '40s. Radio drama and comedy shows began to migrate to TV, causing radio broadcasters to depend on various presentations for entertainment.

The current challenge today has to do with Internet Radio, Satellite Radio, HD Radio, Tablets, and Phone Apps. Gary Begin has touched on all of these eras with his 30 years programming and consulting experience, with the goal of helping students and radio plan for the future. In *Radio Programming and Branding - The Ultimate Podcasting and Radio Programming Guide,* Gary shows broadcasters how to create compelling content and build a listener base.

Can (terrestrial) radio outperform internet and satellite presentations in the future? This book shows how it can with Gary Begin's knowledge and training. *Radio Programming and Branding - The Ultimate Podcasting and Radio Programming*

Guide provides professional methods to succeed in programming, branding (a must!), sales and on-air. Prospering in today's digital world requires hard work, craft, skill, desire, experience and training.

This book is not just a good read for radio station ownership and management, but a very incisive and timely guidebook for students entering the broadcasting profession.

Steve Bianchi
Identity Programming

DEDICATION

This book is dedicated to my wife Pam, who inspired me and helped me through the tough times.

Steve —
Thanks for the Foreward

All My Best —

Gary —

If your radio station can use some programming/promotional/branding assistance, contact Gary Begin of Sound Advantage Media.

gbegin@soundadvantagemedia.com
www.soundadvantagemedia.com
731-437-0536

CHAPTER ONE
HOW TECHNOLOGY AND AUDIO HAVE CHANGED

Y ou moved into your dorm room or new apartment and have begun unpacking the car. The first thing you set up was the stereo system: receiver, turntable or CD player, tape deck and speakers. This all depends upon how old you were at the time. The wires could get tangled, and at times you had to make shelving out of a stack of milk crates. But only when the music was playing on those handpicked CDs, mixtapes or (geezer alert!) vinyl records did you move in the rest of your stuff.

DANIEL RUBIO WOULDN'T KNOW

To the 23-year-old, new dorm rooms and new apartments have meant computers, iTunes, Pandora and miniature speakers.

"All I had to bring was my laptop. That's pretty much what everyone had," says Rubio, who attended Emory University in Atlanta and currently works for a local marketing and communications firm. "It was actually a pretty good sound. It would get the job done."

"Get the job done?" That sounds like the white flag for an era that used to be measured in woofers, tweeters, watts per channel and the size of your record collection (not necessarily in that order).

Indeed, the days of the old-fashioned component stereo system are pretty much over, according to Alan Penchansky, an audiophile and previous columnist for "Billboard," the music trade publication.

"What's happened in the marketplace, the midmarket for audio has completely been obliterated," he says. "You have this high-end market that's getting smaller all the time, and then you've got the convenience market, which has taken over — the MP3s, the Bluetooth devices, playing on laptops."

He wishes more people knew what they were missing. At its best, he says, audio reproduction was "a religious experience."

"There's a primacy to audio," he says. "It's a form of magic."

WIRES AND JACKS

Of course, new technology changes things constantly. When was the last time you bought a roll of film for your camera? Still, for many years — and for a certain, youthful, audience — the stereo system was a point of delight.

Greg Milner, the author of the audio recording history book *Perfecting Sound Forever*, remembers the process. There were components. There were boxes and boxes of tapes and CDs. There might have even been some vinyl.

It could be difficult, no question. The equipment was heavy. There were all those wires, plugs and jacks — Line In, Line Out, Aux, Phono, and CD, keeping track of the positive and negative strands of speaker wire. It was a struggle just to break down and set the stuff up, never mind moving it.

Milner, for example, grew up in Hawaii, and when he went away to school in Minnesota, he had to figure out what he was going to do with his system.

Whole stores were once devoted to stereo components. That hasn't been the case for years.

"I remember agonizing, 'What do I do? I can't take my

stereo,'" he recalls. "There was this thing that, looking back on it, took up a ridiculous amount of psychic energy." However, he observes that the history of audio technology has often been one of suitability.

AUDIOPHILES VS. AM RADIO

During the '50s and '60s, when stereo sound first became widespread, the audiophiles had their hi-fis — and the younger generation listened to tinny AM radios and cheap phonographs.

Indeed, music styles had a lot to do with music consumption, he points out. Audiophiles listened to classical and jazz, music from clubs and concert halls. On a good system, you could hear every pluck of a violin pizzicato, every inflection of a jazz singer's vocals, recreated in your living room.

The kids, on the other hand, listened to basic rock 'n' roll. "The seeds of the decline of what it meant to own a stereo were planted way back then, because the original audiophiles were people who were baby boomers' fathers and mothers," he says. "As rock 'n' roll starts to become more of a thing, a lot of that stuff is produced so it's meant to be heard on AM radios."

According to Milner, A Phil Spector Wall of Sound production — in glorious mono! — would probably have driven a hi-fi enthusiast up a wall.

THE MASS MARKET CONTINUES TO CHANGE

In the '70s and '80s, the two did meet… for a time. Rock and pop music production techniques improved. At the same time, grown-up baby boomers, now working adults, invested in better audio equipment, all the better to listen to Steely Dan's "Aja."

There were whole mass-market stores devoted to audio gear — Sound Trek, Hi-Fi Buys, and Silo — no issue of Rolling Stone was complete without several ads for turntables, cassette decks and equalizers.

But technology marched on, and so did change. Some was for the sake of convenience: Cassettes had more hiss and less range than LPs, but were more portable — especially when listening on your handy Walkman or boom box.

However, we also started focusing more on visuals. Penchansky traces the decline of the stereo system to the early '80s rise of the music video, which brought visuals to the forefront. Suddenly, the concert hall in your living room — or the audio imaging in your head — was gone, replaced by surrealist pictures overpowering the television's small speaker. The sound wasn't as important as the visual. That branch of consumption has helped lead to the home theater.

Penchansky has nothing against HDTVs and 7.1 systems, but believes that, for the most part, it's an "auditory compromise." A pure audio system, "There was no way that television, even today, simulates the realism of visual experience the way (good) audio can simulate an audio experience."

Sure, technology has adjusted. The cream always rises to the top of the bottle.

"New materials and processing technology have improved the sound of small and inexpensive devices," says Patrick Lavelle, president and CEO of the consumer electronics giant VOXX International, which manufactures such brands as Klipsch, Acoustic Research and Advent.

Headphones and an iPod

"Yet there's still a consumer market for good audio," adds Geir Skaaden, an executive at the high-definition audio company DTS. The top-selling products in Apple Stores, after Apple's own devices, are headphones, he says. (DTS recently introduced technology for an immersive system called Headphone: X, intended for mobile devices.)

Still, convenience ultimately rules. Which means it's out with the component system and in with the computer. That suits Rubio fine, who is an Emory graduate. He grew up in a house with a component system but doesn't believe he's missing anything.

"All you need is a good pair of headphones and an iPod and that's pretty much it," he says.

Milner, the author, can't question his decision.

"Now, why even bother?" he asks. "If you can take your entire music collection and more in something that fits in your pocket, why wouldn't you do that?"

CHAPTER TWO
WHAT MAKES A GOOD PROGRAM DIRECTOR?

1. A good radio program director is a tactician. They study the market, assess the competitors' relative strengths and weaknesses, and adjust the station's programming accordingly.

2. A good PD respects the staff and is vigilant to always treat them courteously.

3. A good PD is a perpetual student. The PD is not ignorant enough to think he knows it all.

4. A good PD respects the audience. The PD understands that the radio station's mission is to serve its listeners.

5. A good PD teaches the air staff to respect the audience. He teaches them how to talk to listeners on the phone and at personal appearances. He never speaks disparagingly of listeners, because he knows the air staff will follow his example.

6. A good PD becomes an expert in the community the station serves. Not just the "target demo," but in the community at large: the neighborhoods, the schools, recreation, and local politics.

7. A good PD does not allow anyone else on the staff to mess with the air talents.

Station manager is offended by something a jock said? Tell it to the PD, not to the jock. Salesperson received a complaint from a client about something that happened on-air? Take it to the PD, not the jock.

CHAPTER THREE
RADIO FORMAT GUIDE

RADIO'S MOST POPULAR FORMATS

Format	Count	Format	Count
Country	2037	Adult Hits	188
News/Talk	1359	Urban AC	165
Latin/Hispanic	721	Contemporary Christian	152
Oldies	720	R&B	135
Adult Contemporary	631	Modern Rock	123
Sports	553	Alternative Rock	122
CHR (Top 40)	474	Ethnic	109
Classic Rock	459	Jazz	77
Adult Standards	372	Pre-Teen	57
Hot AC	369	R&B Adult/Oldies	43
Religion (Teaching, Variety)	304	Variety	36
Rock	279	Gospel	30
Soft AC	262	Classical	24
Classic Hits	258	Easy Listening	19
Black Gospel	256	Modern AC	18
Southern Gospel	208	Other/Format Unavailable	9

Total Commercial Stations in Operation – 10569
Number of Stations on the Air Broadcasting in HD – 995
Number of Streaming Radio Stations – 3815

REVIEW OF RADIO FORMATS

Active Rock - The term often used for stations which play rock music designed to be played loudly, such as "hard rock," "metal," and "heavy metal."

Adult Album Alternative (AAA) - A station which plays large-ly current music which tends to appeal more to adults than to teenagers. AAA playlists are much broader than the limited playlists of hit radio, and, therefore, depend on album tracks as well as on music released or designated as singles. Stylistically, such stations may play rock, folk-rock, country-rock, modern rock, blues, folk, and world music. Some publications refer to the adult-oriented rock music heard on AAA stations as "Pro-gressive Rock," not to be confused with the '70s music of the same name.

Adult Alternative - A station which plays current hits, wheth-er single releases or popular album tracks, which tend to ap-peal to adults more than to teenagers. Playlists are drawn from rock, pop, country-rock, folk-rock and blues releases. There are no stations of this type in the New York area.

Adult Contemporary (AC) - A station primarily playing popular and rock music released during the past 15 or 20 years, designed for general listeners rather than for listen-ers actively interested in hearing current releases. The play-lists of many AC stations will also include a limited selec-tion of older material and current hits. See Lite AC, Hot AC, and Rock AC.

Album Oriented Rock (AOR) - This is a format so named as to distinguish itself from Top 40 stations of the past, which played primarily singles. AOR stations thrived between the late '60s and the '80s during the heyday of FM Rock Radio. See Rock, Classic Rock.

Alternative Rock - A station which plays rock music which is stylistically derivative of the Seattle grunge bands of the late '80s, and to some extent, the punk/new wave artists of the late '70s, rather than the "classic" rock artists of the '60s and '70s. These stations are aimed primarily at teenage audiences and feature mostly current single releases and popular album cuts.

Since the Alternative Rock peak of the mid-90s, many alternative rock bands (and stations) have evolved in the direction of modern rock, or in some cases, hard rock. ^{See Modern Rock.}

Americana - A station which plays mostly current country-rock, folk-rock, blues and American roots music which tends to appeal to adults more than to teenagers.

Classic Rock - A station which plays rock music released during the '60s, '70s and '80s. These stations recreate the sound of Album Oriented Rock stations of that period (although often with a much more limited playlist) and appeal mainly to adults rather than to teenagers. Some Classic Rock stations play a limited amount of current releases, stylistically consistent with the station's sound.

Contemporary Hit Radio (CHR) - A station which plays a significant amount of current popular music, whether singles or album cuts. As it is no longer unusual for a single to remain on the charts for 30-40 weeks or longer, "current" refers to music released within the last year. A more accurate description for "CHR" would be "Current Hit Radio." This format is the descendent of the Top 40 stations popular from the '50s through the '80s.

Although some CHR stations base their playlists on surveys of local record sales or phone requests, most rely on published charts such as the Billboard Hot 100. As of December, 1998, the Billboard Hot 100 chart began to include popular album tracks not commercially released as singles, and began weighing a song's airplay three times as heavily as a song's sales. The Billboard Hot 100 chart is, therefore, a measure of which songs are being played on CHR stations which, in turn, base their playlists on Billboard's Hot 100 chart.

Contemporary Hit Radio stations tend to concentrate on specific music styles, such as Rock or Urban, or a range of styles, such as Rock/Pop/Dance or R&B/Rap/Dance. Some

CHR stations play a significant amount of hits released during the past 10 or 15 years, particularly if there are insufficient current hit releases which fall within the station's stylistic range.

Country - Stations that play Contemporary Country, Mainstream Country, Classic Country or any mixture of the above. Due to the overall popularity of Country (the number 1 listened to music in the United States), it's not uncommon to see three or four country stations in a market.

Dance - A station which plays music, whether or not current, produced primarily to be played for dancing. This type of music was originally known as Disco music. Stations which play mostly current Dance music are often referred to as "CHR-Rhythmic," while stations which play Dance music of the past two decades are referred to as "Rhythmic AC."

Ethnic/International - Programs which feature music, whether traditional or popular, of a particular ethnic group, nation, or region, and are aimed at listeners from the featured group or place. Compare to World Music.

Hot Adult Contemporary (Hot AC) - A station which plays commercial popular and rock music released during the past 15 or 20 years which is livelier than the music played on the average Adult Contemporary station, but is still designed to appeal to general listeners rather than listeners interested in hearing current releases.

Another definition of "Hot Adult Contemporary" used in the radio industry is an Adult Contemporary station which plays a significant amount of new rock/pop releases. There is no strict rule as to how much new material a station needs to play in order to be considered "CHR" rather than "Hot AC."

To confuse matters further, you will often see an "Adult Contemporary" music chart, which tracks current songs that appeal to adults but are more pop-oriented than songs found on the "Adult Alternative" chart. Billboard Magazine also compiles an "Adult Top 40" Chart, which tracks rock singles and album cuts which appeal to an adult audience. This chart reflects airplay on rock-oriented CHR stations as well as the new release airplay component of Hot AC stations. See AC, Lite AC, and Rock AC.

Lite Adult Contemporary (Lite AC) - A station playing particularly easy-going popular and rock music released during the past 15 or 20 years, designed to appeal to general listeners. This format is the descendent of the not-quite-extinct "Easy Listening" format of years past.

Modern Rock - A station which plays mostly current rock music performed by artists which have become prominent during the past 5 to 10 years. Stylistically, the music tends to fall between Rock and Alternative Rock. See Alternative Rock, Rock.

Music Formats generally refer to what a radio station's music format sounds like and is governed by four parameters: music style, music time period, music activity level, and music sophistication.

Music Style refers strictly to the type of music played, regardless of how the music is packaged for airplay.

Music Time Period refers to the time of the music's release. "Current" music generally refers to music released within the last year. "Contemporary" music generally refers to music released within the past 15 or 20 years. "Oldies" generally refers to music released between the mid-50s and the mid-70s, and "Nostalgia" refers to music released prior to the mid-50s.

Music Activity Level is a measure of the music's dynamic impact, ranging from soft and mellow to loud and hard-driving. Some names of music styles include built-in descriptions of the music's activity level: "hard rock," "smooth jazz."

Music Sophistication is a reflection of whether the musical structure and lyrical content of the music played is simple or complex. Although difficult to quantify, this factor often determines the composition of a station's audience. It is also reflected in the presentation of the station's air staff.

Oldies - A station which plays popular, rock 'n roll, and rock music released during the "golden era of hit music," roughly 1955-1975. The term "Oldies" is actually a misnomer; a more accurate name for this format would be "Golden Hits," as music from the post-1975 period may qualify as "old" but will rarely qualify as "gold." Across the country, the format of various Oldies stations vary, some playing '50s and '60s music, others '60s, '70s, and even '80s music, '70s music only, "rock oldies," or R&B oldies. A format which became briefly popular in the '90s was the "Jammin' Oldies" format, which featured R&B oldies from the late '60s and '70s.

Personality Programs are formats which rely on the personalities of an on-air host or hosts to entertain listeners, often with humor, parody, satire, or commentary on current events. Personality programming may also include music, interviews, and other features.

Rock - A station which plays mostly current rock music, whether single releases or album cuts. Due to the diversity within rock music today, the playlists of different rock stations will tend to fall within different stylistic ranges. See Modern Rock, Alternative Rock, Active Rock, Rock AC.

Rock AC - A station which plays rock music released largely during the past 15 or 20 years, designed for the general rock listener who is not actively interested in following current releases. These stations, sometimes known as "rock hits," include some "classic rock" material and some current material in their playlists. Some of the "name" formats such as "Jack" include some pop material along with rock hits.

Smooth Jazz - A station which plays easy-going popular music with a "jazzy" feel, designed to set a mood rather than to invite critical listening. "Smooth Jazz" is often set to a medium-tempo or "hip-hop" beat. This format is often referred to as New Adult Contemporary, or "NAC."

Standards/Big Band - A station which plays popular music recorded by the Big Bands of the late '30s and '40s, music recorded by Big Band-era singers during the '40s and '50s, and/or interpretations of the "standards" of that period, including recent interpretations. This format is primarily aimed at older adults and is sometimes referred to as an "Adult Standards" or "Nostalgia" format. Some stations of this type will play any non-rock popular music of the past 60 years.

Talk - A format or program which features one or more hosts discussing current events and other topics, often in the context of a particular political ideology. Talk programs frequently feature in-studio guests and calls from members of the public, representing varying degrees of expertise. Health, medical, and financial topics are especially popular.

Urban Stations - A program which plays music, such as rap, hip-hop, R&B, and soul, in the styles which are the descendants of rhythm & blues music of past decades. The mix favored by any given station depends in large part upon the age of the station's audience. Many Urban stations which appeal to adults rather than to teenagers include soul/R&B hits dating back twenty years or longer, and are sometimes characterized as "Urban AC."

World Music - Programs which play music that evoke musical styles of one or more regions of the world; the music does not necessarily have to be performed by musicians from those regions or aimed solely at listeners from those regions. Compare Ethnic/International Music.

*Other Music Formats - Other popular music station formats include Jazz, Classical, and Spanish. In some parts of the country, there are sub-categories within these formats.

CHAPTER FOUR
MORNING SHOW BASICS

• Become part of their routine – Research tells us that regular morning listening is part of a pattern. Fitting into your listener's routine is essential. You do that with content delivered at the right times and some content that might be segregated from times when younger ears are present (think of mom driving the kids to school).

• Weather, traffic, and news headlines trump celebrity news and gossip. It goes back to what listeners need to know to feel prepared, and Justin Bieber's latest prank isn't necessary for most listeners.

• Music is the best weapon in morning drives, but that alone will not win the battle. Most people tune in for a "lift" with music, so watch the overall tempo.

• Likewise, mood is critical, as the need for a lift involves content and how talents deliver it. Watch the negativity. Listeners want to feel good.

• Reality-type content looks good in the latest research, including prank calls (watch the legal aspects of these). Trivia remains popular.

• Local content is good, because listeners won't get that online in most cases. Local info is not the driving force, however. As with news, it's "what's most important right now" that counts.

• There's a "keep me on time" aspect as listeners use radio to time their morning progress. That's why being "on time" with benchmarks like news is so important. Do you really want to make your listener late to work? The older the listener, the more likely they are to wake up with you using a clock radio. Younger listeners tune in less automatically, and you may be one of their many morning habits (checking email, downing caffeine, etc.).

• Companionship is foremost. Radio may be the only voice that talks to that listener in the morning!

CHAPTER FIVE
HOW TO INCREASE MORNING RATINGS

1. Commit to a weekly planning/brainstorming meeting.
Everyone connected to the show from interns to PDs should attend this meeting. Use 100% of the available creative brainpower at your station. At the meeting, everyone is responsible for bringing in multiple ideas from categories like: phone topics, personal stories, games, new features, guests/interviews, production piece (song parody, etc.), promotion, stunt idea, serial story line, web/viral content idea, etc.

2. Make imaging the show a priority.
Imaging speeds up the process of familiarizing people with the show, for both new and established shows. Many people cume the radio station yet may not listen to the morning show. Make the promos a priority as opposed to being the last thing the show does before flying out the door. We can help you brainstorm ideas on how to best promote your show.

3. Asking is better than telling.
An effective way to start a difficult conversation with an employee or coworker is by asking a question. Often a personality or employee will know themselves when and even why something didn't work. If you start with "That sucked!" or "Why did you do that?!" the person feels defensive immediately. By asking a question, like "How do you think that [break] went?"

The person has the opportunity to learn from their mistake by taking responsibility. "I know. I hated that break." Then you can follow up with questions like, "What can [we/you] do differently next time?" and the person is still with you in the conversation, not mentally on the phone with their therapist.

4. Create more anticipation for content by mastering the art of the tease.

When you pose a question that creates mystery -- or what scientific studies call an information gap in the brain -- it arouses people's curiosity and they feel compelled to find the answer or the resolution. So the purpose of teasing is twofold: One: to retain listeners through each segment of the show. Two: to create a mystery or create an information gap that engages listeners emotionally. It breaks down to: mystery (the information gap) + resolution (fill information gap) = ratings (more listeners).

Raise a question (create mystery/set up an information gap) for every segment of the show, including every phone topic, show feature, guest and appearance by the show or individual players. Listeners will feel like they're going to miss something if they aren't listening.

THERE ARE TWO TYPES OF TEASING:

#1) Vertical teasing is for content that is coming up later in that day's show.

#2) Horizontal teasing is for content you're doing at the same time on future days. You can be confident that most of the people listening at 7:45 am on Tuesday are listening at 7:45 am on another morning. Add a column to the show's run sheet that includes a "coming up in the next couple of days."

Horizontal sells should be longer and more exaggerated than vertical sells. It is not too much to spend three minutes selling something that is going to happen at the same time later in the week.

5. **Take an improv class**.

Improv sharpens listening skills, builds confidence, gets the creative juices flowing, teaches you how to build and expand the content and conversations, improves team rapport and bantering skills. Maybe most importantly, it stretches you and gives you practice being out of your comfort zone. The less guarded you are, the more your authentic personality can come through. And believe it or not: it helps not just talent, but also producers and even managers, to find their comedic voice and to loosen up.

CHAPTER SIX
BECOMING A PERSONALITY ON A
MUSIC INTENSIVE RADIO STATION

You need radio personalities for audience connection, just as you need forward momentum for audience preservation. It's not easy to dodge the fact that listeners perceive your personality talking as an interruption. I have some thoughts on how to integrate speech breaks in your music playlist.

Music radio listeners don't like sudden changes, when music ends and talk (minus background music) commences. Consider using a talk over bed. It will keep your station in the flow while increasing TSL. You'll create an affirmative music aura for your brand if you preserve a coherent impression of non-stop music.

Talking over intros is a way to construct music flow. Allow your Creative Services Director or Imaging Director to produce intros for songs that don't have one initially and request record labels for instrumental versions so you may use an appropriate piece for your tailor-made radio edit. This will aid with increased Time Spent Listening.

Operating a talk bed or jingle ramp is another way to uphold music drive. Your station imaging will also keep the energy level of your personality breaks as announcers naturally regulate their rhythm of speaking to the mood of the music. Sporadically, it can be useful to discard background music to get listeners' full attention, or just because it's appropriate.

It's crucial to build consistent rhythm and flow. A talk break can be a wonderful way to aid in building an impressive music image. When you design your program clock dependably, you'll teach listeners that, on your station, talk is followed by a great deal of music. They will learn this after repeated listening. You also want to use a consistent music and talk ratio, such as one song, short talk, two songs, and longer talk. This rhythm is another familiar design. It sounds minimal, but these things add up to make your station sound comprehensive while being unlike the competition - even if you play exactly the same format.

One half of radio programming is science while the other is human art. If you find yourself on a music intensive station, try making your breaks interesting and engaging by talking less while saying more. It's not how much you say, but what you say that brings listeners to your station. Become more than just a liner jock. If you combine creative imagination with editorial skills (less is more), you'll be combining science and art.

CHAPTER SEVEN
TEN STAGES TO A MORE EFFECTIVE RADIO AIR CHECK AND CRITIQUE SESSION

For Program Directors to be successful air talent coaches, it's important to stop thinking in terms of the process as a critique, but rather as advice. It is critical to do the following:

1. Ascertain Vital Subjects.
Take the time to get out of the station and listen to the CD of your talent's shows. Listening in real time does not allow you to go back and hear breaks a second or third time. Once you've stopped listening to the CD, make a request list of the vital issues you'd like to address with that air personality.

2. Arrange Issues by Impression.
Ask yourself this question: which one issue will ensure improvement in the air personality's ratings beginning today? Start your coaching session with the items on the top of your list.

3. Choose one or two vital subject issues.
Pick no more than two issues to work on in each advice session. Don't bring a long laundry list of issues to the air check session involving minutia with what is really important. People have a hard enough time dealing with change overall. The more changes you ask for at one time, the less likely you'll get any.

4. Identify Objectives.

Radio Air Personalities perform on the air with good intentions. Sadly, as they say, the way to hell is paved with good intentions. We all can have good intentions and obtain bad results. One of the ways to understand why the air personality is performing in a way you wish to change is to prevent defensive behavior from arising during your coaching session. Once you express understanding for your air talent's good intentions, it demonstrates you see them as well-meaning people.

5. Search for "Big Picture" Perspective.

How you present each coaching point will do the most for determining the success or failure of offering advice. Make sure you think this part of the process through very carefully before each coaching session. Try to find a way to direct your coaching points that establishes the big picture of building ratings, revenue, community good will, etc. One of the most common challenges Program Directors experience with air talent is too much material or words crammed into single sets. Outlining this issue from the perspective of the listeners and how challenging it is for them to comprehend unfocused sets makes it much easier to understand why improved editing matters.

6. Formulate Details.

Transcribe at least one hour of the talent's show on paper for each coaching session. Once you transcribe, you've accomplished two things. First, you have indisputable evidence of what occurred on the air. Highly creative people, such as radio air talent, are always focused on the future. They have no clear sense of what happened in the past. The second thing you accomplish with transcription has to do with basic human emotion. When we comprehend words on paper, we need to use the part of our brains that's rooted in logic. This helps avoid occurrences of emotional hijacking from happening as often as air check sessions.

7. Construct Your Example.

Examine your transcriptions and choose several examples which support your coaching point. If you only bring one example, you run the risk of being rebuffed with a response like, "Well, you just picked a bad break." Collect any other data that supports your point. One of the big components of advice is the perception of your level of expertise.

8. Think Progression, Not Product.

During your coaching sessions, think in terms of changing the talent's progression, not their product. Concentrate on possibilities rather than solutions. When you change the procedure, the product follows. Learning over a lifetime occurs when we change how someone thinks. No one wishes to be told exactly how to do their job.

9. Presume Success.

Approach every coaching session with the presumption that what you've asked the talent will happen on the air. Say to them things like, "I have total faith in your talent and abilities and know you'll make this happen on your show." This requires a leap of faith for programmers, but people tend to rise or fall in an organization contingent upon how management treats them. If you treat people as though they cannot fail, they rarely do. If they're treated as if they can never succeed, they never will.

10. Screen for Progress.

After every coaching session, make a sincere effort to find your talent doing something right. Too much criticism de-motivates people and will cause what I call "Creative Paralysis." Suitable encouragement for progress and praise is your most powerful and cheapest motivational tool. Too many managers don't take the time to use it. Taking the time to notice alone will help make you a more efficient radio air talent coach.

CHAPTER EIGHT
DEFINING YOUR RADIO STATION'S UNIQUE LISTENING PROPOSITION

Ask yourself: why should a listener in your target audience listen to YOUR Radio Station at any given moment vs. the competition? You can extend that by saying vs. anything else as well - including turning off the radio.

List everything done on your Radio Station on a daily basis (on the air). I mean everything!

• We solicit phone calls
• We talk to listeners
• We sweep our quarter hours
• We ask trivia questions

Don't just list features - catalogue the things you do on your Radio Station performed repeatedly.

• We tease across all breaks
• We tease upcoming newscasts
• We provide weather checks
• We pound our station name into listeners' heads
• We talk about the music
• We perform dedications
• We give showbiz news
• We plug the Radio Station website often

- We inform listeners how to contact the station
- We provide contest details
- We solicit listener criticism
- We mention the names of contest winners
- We inquire as to what listeners are doing
- We try to stump the sports or newscaster with sports trivia
- We provide artist information
- We mention listener birthdays
- We mention celebrity birthdays

When you "brainstorm," the answers come at the end of the session. It's not the material on-top, but the substance you must push for. Now, we're going to examine the ways to take what you wrote down and proceed to make them larger than life for your audience.

If you start answering your on-air phone calls by saying, "Hi, who's this?" this is NOT a unique listening proposition. It could be coming from any Radio Station in town. You must discover a way to answer your on-air phone calls that brands it as your Radio Station.

"Hi, what do your friends call you?" Sounds more like a private club. Brand it so it sounds original, real and relatable. Doesn't need to be brilliant if it's original, real and relatable. Just original!

How do you end your phone calls? Do you end them the same way as every other personality at the station, or did you create a unique and interesting method? NEVER DO: "What's your favorite Radio Station?"

Time Checks --- When you give the time, can you create a way that listeners know they're listening to YOUR Radio Station? Can you *whisper* the calls? Work with a child to record your call letters. With all the big-balls imaging out there, what do you think will stand out?

If you give showbiz news, call it "Tabloid Trash." Brand it on your own terms. Do custom jingles mentioning the outskirt towns. Rotate them. Appear as if you're including everybody. Obligate a staff member to compile a list of local pubs and bars. When someone calls, ask the caller, "How's everyone down at_____ tonight or this afternoon?" This makes you sound "plugged-in." This might be better used during an afternoon drive or evening show.

Have a list of area High School mascots in your listening area. This takes a lot more prep on the personalities part but how powerful is it when someone calls and asks, "Hey, how are the Cougars doing?" Your response can be, "The Cougars are playing the Wildcats tonight. Who are you rooting for?"

Remember: preparing is caring. You'll sound as if you know everything about your listeners. Understand what your audience does. When you promote the Radio Station website, give your listeners a reason to go see it. "To sign up for our contest *'Beat the Toaster,'* you must sign up on our website." "When we call your name at 7:20 every weekday morning, you'll have ten minutes to call us back. We put the toast in and you must come up with the answer to our trivia question before the toast pops up." "Answer correctly and receive a $500 dollar gas card."

It's very relatable, fun, and different. Your listeners know what a toaster is. Extremely visual and completely ridiculous. If another station in your market plays *"Beat the Toaster,"* they'll seem pretty foolish. To hear *"Beat the Toaster,"* you can only be listening to _____. It must seize the attention of your listeners. The more you can make a feature your own (Branding), the more you stand out from the crowd.

CHAPTER NINE
PUT ME IN, COACH! I'M READY TO PLAY

Effective Coaching Helps 'Push' Business Success and 'Pull' Effective Leadership.

If you're not getting better, you're falling behind. In today's multi-media world, you need to "take your game to the next level."

To be competitive, you need effective coaching.

Tiger Woods knows this, as does every world class athlete, opera singer, performer or executive. It's true of your station sales, programming, technical and other staff as well.

Winners in any profession understand that without the right "coach," they won't achieve their objectives. And the objective is winning.

As a consultant, I must wear many hats: advisor, expert, salesperson, problem solver, coach, referee, banker, publisher and author. I believe a steady focus on effective coaching will increase your performance, even in the face of client and project distractions; it will also secure your spot as a winner.

Active ongoing coaching is the quickest way to improve your station's performance level. Unfortunately, coaching may be the item bypassed by busy general managers, market managers, programmers, DOEs and sales managers.

In my travels as a consultant, I am reminded every time I turn on the radio that most air talent lack the "relate-ability" and entertainment skills necessary to keep me tuned in.

Since coaching is something done *with* people, rather than *to* people, how well prepared (both in skills and attitude) are managers to coaches? Managers typically possess an innate interpersonal technique, so perhaps management's perceived value of coaching can be an indication of how readily it's being absorbed into business culture and put into practice.

Coaching has a powerful, long-term impact on people and your station's effectiveness. Coaching is talking with a person in a way that helps him or her solve a problem.

Some managers confuse coaching with giving advice. As Gore Vidal said, "There is no human problem which could not be solved if people would simply do as I advise."

The reality is often that, as Gordon Dickson noted, "Some people like my advice so much that they frame it upon the wall instead of using it."

What is a more effective approach?

Managers are asked to improve productivity without additional resources. They need to invite employees to participate as partners, develop trusting relationships and combine everyone's best efforts into creating business solutions.

One option is to enhance behavior and performance through interactive communication and influence, such as coaching. Managers also need to use their coaching skills within the company with those who don't necessarily report to them, and are outside their organization. There is an increasing need to improve involvement and engagement of all employees to achieve business outcomes.

An effective coaching skills strategy emphasizes collaboration and respect rather than control and faultfinding. Such a strategy adds a tangible aspect of value. People can see effort being expanded in helping them do a good job and experiencing a sense of achievement. Effective coaching skills, therefore, contribute to not only a "push" to achieving business outcomes, but also a "pull" towards effective leadership.

TRAITS

What makes a good management coach?

Think of the following as an "air-check" for your management team on coaching employees.

Knows the discipline he or she is coaching.

It seems obvious, but a coach must know the ins and outs of the discipline — the rules, the history, the tactics, etc. Without it, neither coach nor employee will be able to do their jobs properly and will quickly lose face when they start making mistakes.

Motivates the team.

This is probably the most important trait of a good coach. Without proper motivation, everything comes apart. Remember that a coach will need to lead a team of individuals; each individual has different personal goals. The coach's job is giving the team enough motivation to turn their attention from their private matters to the goals of the station.

Talks only when it gets results.

A good coach will never speak without a good cause. If he or she talks too much, employees will stop listening. A coach should talk only when necessary — this will give their words extra weight.

Ability to listen.

Being calmer than usual is a good indication the coach is a good listener. If the manager is to become a good coach, he or she needs to think like a surrogate father or mother for the team; listening is the single most important trait that can make it possible.

Knows their team.

Another important matter is a coach knowing one's team. It's not only about matching numbers with names. A good coach knows about the professional and the private lives of their teammates.

Treats everyone individually.
While a good coach should know everybody, it is necessary to treat each employee individually. Treat them as you would like to be treated.

Leads by example.
A good coach does everything he or she will ask others to do. They always set an example.

INTERPERSONAL ISSUES

Beyond technical aspects of setting goals during coaching, it is critical to pay attention to certain interpersonal issues: As a coach, you must set clear expectations, performance standards and specific objectives regarding what should be done, when and how. Measure performance. Focus on behavior, not value judgments. Correct deviations from performance standards.

Make it clear that you are on the same side as the employee and that the objective of the meeting is for the employee to be successful. Provide guidance while preserving the employee's self-esteem. Give an employee with longer service an extended time to improve. Set the time for improvement in accordance with the specific behavior involved.

Managers, employees and their established work practices, are under pressure to change and achieve results never before asked of them. Effective coaching skills, while not the only need, can be a major contributor to the solutions.

Effective systematic coaching is an opportunity to build meaningful partnerships between members of an organization who meet these challenges. Without effective coaching skills, progress is just that much harder.

Mark Twain said it best: "I'm all for progress, its change that I don't like."

CHAPTER TEN
"EMOTIONALLY BRANDING YOUR RADIO STATION"

Branding is not only about ubiquity, visibility, and functions; it's about bonding emotionally with listeners. Only when your station kindles an emotional dialogue with listeners, can your radio station qualify as a brand. Listeners want to deal with radio stations that are responsive and sensitive to their unique needs. When effectively executed, "branding" increases a radio station's market share and profitability by leveraging awareness while clearly positioning the station. In layman's terms: to attract listeners, Program Directors must think like listeners.

For branding to be truly effective, radio stations have to feel and sound dead-on with their listener's expectations. The correct mixture of language, sounds and expressions will accomplish this. You need to stand for something to stand out from the crowd. Radio stations must become strong brands. It's termed a culture: a set of beliefs and expectations celebrated and enjoyed every day. A distinctive experience listeners want to become part of.

As radio's background has changed so dramatically in the new millennium with the advent of listening options such as internet radio, satellite, HD, tablets and smartphones, the audience must care about what is said. It has to matter to them. It has to touch their lives in some significant way. As we are in the middle part of the second decade of the new millennium, broadcast radio (the original portable medium), persists to dominate in spite of newer, aggressive audio technologies.

The fact that you can listen to radio while doing something else is the reason it maintains its popularity. Radio can never stop innovating. That will become its death knell. For your radio station to be very successful, you must constantly anticipate new developments and freshen your productivity.

Make sure your station has a unique USP in your market that draws listeners and keeps them entertained. Establish your brand and maintain a high quality. Remember: perception is reality. If and how long people tune into your station mainly depends on their impression of your station — your image — which is based on previous listening experiences. Develop positive brand images with the listener!

Keep transforming your radio station. Try and anticipate where the market will be, say, five years from now. Don't make many moves that will distort your audience and damage your brand. Invest in talent development and coaching while searching for tomorrow's radio personalities. Give fresh talents a chance but make sure they relate to your station's target audience. Make sure your radio personalities are natural storytellers. Great storytellers make a nice story great by the way they present it.

Build distinctive and familiar brands. Create a brand for your radio station where people feel at home, through imaging, marketing and events. You're more than just a radio station; you're a brand! Create a brand that your audience can relate to; make sure they know what to expect. This goes way beyond music. It's about a shared feeling. Radio is a great medium to embrace new developments. Apply innovation to the complete output of your station, from programming to marketing.

Now that the music industry's impact has deteriorated, record companies are not the only jumpstart for talent: with radio and social media combined, you can create an enormously important and fun place to work by branding your station as the place that plays the latest music. Music discovery is still dominated by radio, although teens now turn to YouTube and iTunes to discover new music.

Most radio programmers agree that constant innovation, familiar brands and shared emotion are key to securing radio's future in today's social media world. The technology and content behind radio offers all the possibilities in the world. Radio is immediate, live and fast. The final conclusion? Radio brands will continue to thrive on emotion and a personal relation with the listener.

CHAPTER ELEVEN
STAND BY YOUR BRAND

"Make one point."
"Make it simple."
"Make it something worth listening to."

Sounds easy, doesn't it? Find out what people want and give it to them. A recipe for success! Unfortunately, most radio stations are anything but simple. In my travels as a consultant, it's amazing the number of stations that make listeners jump through hoops to listen. Too much "clutter" in stop sets and too many positioners creates confusion for the listener. It's a recipe for disaster!

We need to start thinking of our listeners as "customers." The better we're able to understand how our listeners "consume" our product, the better we'll be able to market, package and produce a product acceptable to the marketplace. In essence, programmers need to become "brand managers" of their radio stations.

We live in an over-communicated society. For a radio station to succeed in such a crowded environment, the station must create a position in the listener's mind. That position must take into account not only its own strengths and weaknesses, but those of the competition as well. When we think of computers, most people think of IBM, but IBM didn't invent the computer - Sperry-Rand did. IBM was the first company to build a computer position in the mind of the consumer. Radio needs to do the same thing! Build a position in the listener's mind that you're a station with instant top-of-mind awareness.

Two Types of Customers

Radio is unique in that it has two types of customers; listeners and advertisers. Most companies don't suffer from that phenomenon. Their customers are their customers. Radio has to 'sell' its product to listeners on a daily basis. As the marketplace becomes even more fragmented with iPods, Internet radio, mp3s, CDs, satellite and now HD radio, it's the "brands" that people remember --- the thing that makes it comfortable for people to go out, buy and listen to.

The radio dial is filled with more choices than ever before. Listeners are consuming our product on a daily basis. You better be able to stand out in a crowd! The primary reason to create a great product is to create great revenue. The better the product serves and entertains the target listener, the better the opportunity to increase ratings and revenue!

Building Brand Loyalty

Brand loyalty is the Holy Grail for all brand marketers. It's a lot of hard work to establish and maintain that relationship. There is a reward, and it's given to radio stations that develop a successful consumer product relationship with the listener. As programmers, we need to connect with people and develop a sense of 'satisfaction' the listener can embrace. We need to know and understand listeners' beliefs, attitudes and perceptions of our station. We're in the entertainment business; let's capture their imagination. Be creative!

Entertainment Value

Most of the 'fun' has gone out of the radio business. It's become too homogenized, formulated, computerized, and centralized. Radio needs to bring back the 'art' and 'fun' the industry once enjoyed. This all plays into building a brand:

> 1. To create a brand, we must create a unique brand identity communicating our benefits.
> 2. Once the identity is established, we need to build awareness of our brand.
> 3. Create brand loyalty.

Brands live in a highly competitive world. A brand may stand apart, but rarely does it stand alone. Your brand needs to push against commonality, driving a wedge between itself and your competitors. You must become a category of one. Miller Brewing accomplished this by hitting on a unique brand concept: "Tastes Great, Less Filling." Miller Lite found a way to appeal to the rational and emotional sides of beer drinkers at the same time: only Miller Lite could claim to be lower in calories (rational) while offering the taste beer drinkers wanted (emotional). Your radio station needs to accomplish the very same thing.

Over Simplify Your Message: The most effective approach to take in our over-communicated society is the over-simplified message. Less is more. We need to sharpen our message to cut through the clutter. Jettison the ambiguities, simplify the message, and then simplify it even more. That way, you'll make a long-lasting memorable impression. Do you really think listeners believe we're playing "a better mix of music?" Better than what, my iPod?

Drop the things you can't brag about. Instead, brag about what you do best and forget the rest. Cut the crap and focus on making your strengths stronger! Stop insulting your listener with meaningless phrases they don't believe. Relate to your audience. Find out what your strengths are and master them.

Doing so builds a solid reputation and a following. Become known for doing great work in some area rather than mediocre work in a lot of areas.

You Look Marvelous

It's important to come up with a signature style. Producer Phil Spector was sought out in the '60s by the Beatles and Rolling Stones for his unique "Wall of Sound." His track record included producing such hits as "Be My Baby" and "You've Lost That Lovin' Feeling" by creating a dense, complex, "everything-and-the-kitchen-sink" type of sound. He mastered what he did and people wanted to work with him.

Come up with a strong theme. Do your best to be entertaining, thought provoking and memorable. Develop bits that the audience will enjoy and remember. This will become your signature that no one in your market will be able to copy. Listeners don't know what they like, but like what they know. Brand yourself in a way the audience can relate and embrace, and any recipe for disaster will soon be the ingredient for success!

CHAPTER TWELVE
HOW TO DEVELOP YOUR PERSONAL BRAND

Possessing a personal brand means showcasing your career accomplishments. If it helps, think of your career as one long brand campaign that will evolve over time but always has the goal of presenting you in the best possible light.

A brand is, in essence, a promise of a certain level of performance. Great brands have high expectations attached to them, and everything associated with a great brand reflects those expectations.

What do the things associated with you say about your personal brand? Seemingly small details add up to a big overall impression. Here are some ways to develop your personal brand.

1. Your written professional bio.

Less formal than a résumé, this document describes your professional value proposition (PVP). It tells readers what's in it for them by letting them know how you benefit them. When they read the PVP, they'll know why they should hire you because of your professional assets.

2. Your elevator speech.

This is the spoken version of your bio. Can you sum up and explain your PVP in 30 seconds or less? If not, practice,

practice, and practice until you can. Give this real thought, because often it is the first impression you'll make on potential employers.

3. Your self-description.
Can you sum up your PVP in just two to four words? Great brands can, and you should be able to do so, as well. Aim to intrigue listeners enough to want to know more about you. Saying "I'm a scientific accountant" is boring. Saying "I'm a numbers detective" is much better.

4. Your business card.
Even if you are not employed and are in the middle of a career change, you need a business card. You can get 500 cards online for little to no cost. Make sure your contact info is on the card and on the back, your brief self-description.

5. Your appearance.
Do you look professional during job interviews? Are you well groomed and dressed appropriately for the organization? It's amazing how many job candidate sabotage themselves by ignoring these basics.

6. Your behavior.
Do you act professional during job interviews? Do you avoid chewing gum and interrupting the person speaking to you? Take a good look at how you behave. Your actions should always reinforce your PVP, not take away from it.

7. Your own domain name.
Find out whether your first name, middle initial, and last name can be strung together as the address for a website. Use a domain registrar like GoDaddy or Active-Domain to find out if it's available. If yes, register it, or some variation of it. Free or low-cost services like Weebly and many others can aid you in building a professional looking website and host it. Make sure that website address is also on your business card.

8. Your social media profiles.

You want a business profile on LinkedIn. Then you want to assess your non-business-oriented profiles on other sites. If there is anything that might embarrass you if a current or potential employer finds it, do your best to clean it up. On Facebook, for example, you may want to unfriend connections that have posted dubious comments or other material. Whom are you following on Twitter? That says more about you than you may realize.

9. Your photo.

Make your headshot photo consistent across the Internet, including your personal website and your social media profiles. This photo is a professionally taken headshot of you alone, dressed in business attire and smiling.

10. Your voice.

Consider starting a blog. You can make it part of your personal website. Commit to posting at least once a week and choose intelligent observations or articles as the basis for your discussion. The point is to establish you as an expert on the Web that people in your industry or field find interesting enough to read regularly.

With regular attention and persistence, your personal brand will become known for quality and even innovation, making you a desirable job candidate or valued employee.

CHAPTER THIRTEEN
GETTING LISTENERS TO LIKE YOUR BRAND

How do you change people's attitude? This is an issue you must address at some point during an ad campaign, a sales pitch, or when you are trying to get people simply to feel better about your radio station.

In the hierarchy of communication effects, achieving a good brand attitude comes after getting a listener's attention and giving him or her knowledge about your brand. But knowledge isn't enough, because people must ultimately like your station's product to listen to it. Getting people to like your product is just a layman's term for what is called a good attitude.

HIGH INVOLVEMENT/LOW INVOLVEMENT AND RATIONAL VS. EMOTIONAL APPEALS

How to achieve a good brand attitude is, in fact, rather complex. But to make it simple, we can break it down into some basic steps. The first step is to determine whether what you sell is a high involvement or low involvement for your radio station or group.

Think of a high involvement product as one that is risky and important for listeners. If you sell a product that is mission critical to a listener (that is, if it doesn't work, the customer's business doesn't work), then it is clearly a high involvement product. Alternatively, low involvement products are not that important or risky to listeners.

A decision must be made about how you will influence the listener's attitude. Two broad ways exist for doing this. One is through a rational persuasion approach; the other is through an emotional appeal. In fact, you see these different types of approaches used all the time in television and print advertising.

How you make this decision depends on what you know about your listeners. If you were trying to change an engineer's attitude, for example, a rational approach would typically (but not always) be best. An artist might be approached more with an emotional appeal. The more you know about your listeners, the easier this decision will be.

With an understanding of the nature of your listener's involvement and the approach you will take, it is relatively easy to see the different strategies that should be used to achieve a good brand attitude.

As an example, consider trying to change the attitude of a listener who is very involved in the product and appears susceptible to rational persuasion. You should use multiple facts, expert and credible sources, scientific evidence, etc.

CHAPTER FORTEEN
WELCOME TO NO-BRAND LAND

Broadcasting executives spend millions building their radio station's brand in the marketplace. But, is it being spent it in the right place?

A marketer's greatest asset in creating brand justice and impact is the frontline sales person. But if you ask Brand Managers for a look at their brand-building budgets, you'd probably see expenses allocated entirely opposite to what really drives brand purchase decisions.

Brand marketers continue to pump big bucks into big ad campaigns while doing next to nothing to deliver relevant, brand-supporting messages at the all-important larger level— the distance between a company's sales voice and a prospect's purchase decision.

What's the answer?

It probably lies somewhere between (1) the unwillingness of radio stations and brand managers to go further "downstream" with their strategic recommendations and (2) the lack of useful tools to get them there. Welcome to No Brand's Land

Increasingly, a company's branding success depends less on what they sell, and more on how they sell it. Selected experts in branding seem to be coming around that the power to make or break your brand-building effort lies not in the quality of your advertising but in the customer's experience at the point of sale. In radio, that's your over-the-air product and how your ad-rep handles the advertiser.

On one side of No Brand's Land, brand marketers can control all of the implementation, ensuring the advertising campaign is right on, the media coverage generated by your on-air promotion is consistent, your Web site looks the same, and your corporate design are in place.

But on the other side of the No Brand's Land, sales people are still doing their own thing. They are cutting and pasting from old proposals with outdated information and incorrect messages. They're fabricating homegrown collateral tools and PowerPoint presentations that are, at best, inconsistent with corporate positioning, or worse, downright inaccurate. Most frightening for brand marketers is that these cobbled-together documents have to walk the halls of prospective customers, representing the company's brand at the most critical points in the sales process. Ouch.

Adding insult to injury, the field-fabrication virus spreads exponentially as this bad information is perpetuated across the channel on the brand's intranet.

Crossing Over No Brand's Land

To effectively navigate and successfully cross No Brand's Land, marketers need to start by adapting brand message creation and delivery to today's strategic sales processes. Two trends in particular will drive marketers' efforts to create brand-supporting content that helps sales people sell.

Trend #1: Value Selling

For more than a decade, sales training and methodology experts have focused on improving the consultative selling skills of sales people—especially in complex selling environments. The concept is simple: first, sales people identify the needs of customers; then, they clearly demonstrate the ability of a solution to successfully respond to that customer's specific needs.

Often called Value Selling or Solution Selling, this dynamic and interactive sales process replaces previously static, one-way techniques that debated the merits of competing features and functions. While sales people move toward creating a much more customized sales experience for each prospect, most marketing departments continued to deliver generic messaging using static collateral tools—a one-size-fits-all approach for a one-to-one world. No wonder sales people are forced to scramble to create their own custom content, piecemealed from various sources, in order to demonstrate they have listened to the customer.

The first thing brand managers can do to help out is translate their high-level positioning into street-ready value propositions and solution-messaging that speak to customers the way sales people have been trained to sell:

> • Create customer empathy by identifying and demonstrating a true understanding of the key do-or-die issues facing your customers. Do that for each level of the decision-making team, and link it back to how they do their jobs today.

> • Next, determine and articulate the risks if they do not address these issues. Also, firmly establish and highlight the rewards if they do take action. Take special care to find out how your customer will define success—determine what they want to brag about if they are successful in achieving positive results.

> • Then demonstrate how your company's solution helps them respond specifically—and successfully—to their key do-or-die issues.

Trend #2: Dynamic, Personalized Collateral Building

Value selling has raised the bar, changing customer expectations about sales experiences forever. Customers have come to expect that company interactions will be personal and relevant, and tailored to their specific needs. Meanwhile, marketing departments have tried to keep pace by adopting segmentation strategies, doing their best to tailor messages and create more customer-relevant positioning. However, the tools to deliver these increasingly sophisticated messages through the sales channels have lagged. So, we've seen a proliferation of static collateral tools designed to fit every occasion.

Unfortunately, sales people are neither warehouse managers nor librarians, and they have a hard time tracking and finding the right materials when they need them. In response, marketers have set up sales intranets to supply 24×7 accesses to support materials.

While these intranets improve accessibility to materials, they don't resolve the biggest issue facing today's value-selling sales people: the need to provide prospects with dynamic, personalized sales communications. With only static documentation at their disposal, sales people begin creating unique, customized documents for each sales situation. Typically, this happens at the expense of the brand and the company. The lack of consistency between radio stations and from sales person to sales person—undermines the millions spent on brand awareness advertising. The extra time spent by sales people to craft these personalized proposals, presentations and collateral pieces keeps them from time better spent with customers.

Marketing's big win is that every radio sales person, even within a multi-entertainment environment, will now be communicating a consistent company message. Imagine the brand-building power unleashed when sales reps begin delivering a persuasive, powerful and pre-approved message at every point of customer contact.

CHAPTER FIFTEEN
REMEMBER ME? — HOW TO GET DIARY KEEPERS TO WRITE DOWN YOUR NAME

You need to produce benchmark features—really memorable items the audience can embrace and remember. Are you doing things that are predictable, mundane, or boring? Or, are you "**Branding**" your features? Making it a part of your personality and the station sets you apart from the rest and helps get you remembered and more importantly, *written down!*

Stations need to seriously re-think their on-air imaging. They are **so forgettable.**

Everyone and his brother have big lasers and ballsy voices. As Nielsen diary keepers go across the dial, you think they're going to remember the bells and whistles? Or, will they remember and write down a station that is entertaining, interesting, and funny, has drama and plays well with the listener? **You** be the judge!

Radio is in the *memory business.* Until PPM or some other methodology is realized full-time in all markets, getting diary keepers to write you in their diaries will largely depend on remembering your stations name, frequency or uniqueness. **Something that singles you out and gets your station written down!** This is not the time to be shy. Creating memorable experiences or features (like "The Five O'clock Funnies"), increases your chances over time of increasing diary entries.

The part of radio's **"magic"** is the fact that we do things our listeners cannot do themselves! Our listeners don't have traffic helicopters, news staffs, meteorologists, sports reporters, huge cd libraries. They don't interview important people or give away great prizes. **We** get to do that! You know what **they** can do?

They can turn the dial! So take material you or someone else has created and make it your own. Unique, memorable experiences are a large part of what gets you remembered and more importantly, *written down!*

Great radio stations and personalities pull you along effortlessly. The listeners don't lose their interest. That's because there's a great natural **flow** to the station.

Flow is what helps build TSL and keeps you from suffering from listener fatigue.

You want to build flow because it helps to make a show a series of discreet elements rather than separate, disjointed features.

Every time a personality says *"Now it's time for"* or *"we'll be back after this,"*

you're subconsciously telling the listener that whatever reason they came to you no longer exists. What you're hearing is an **exit.** The real message is it's OK to leave. The problem is you can't *come back* unless *you leave!* Makes sense, doesn't it? Don't give your audience permission or a reason to leave. That makes for greater TSL and more opportunity for diary keepers to *write down* your station.

Do everything you can to get as much cume as possible from your target demo. This is especially important when running contests on-air. Contests are not about winning; they're an excuse to enjoy the relationship you already have with your listeners. That means furnishing a reason for your listeners to *"stick around."*

Every time you ask your listeners to do something, they silently ask themselves *"why?"* "What's in it for me?" "Is there something interesting to do?" "Something fun and exciting?"

If you can't answer those questions, chances are your listeners can't either. Whatever you do **has** to be worth listening to; if it isn't **don't** put it on-the-air.

I'm a big believer in placing your **exact frequency** in all your station's branding.

After all it **is** your name. We live in a digital world and your audience "gets it."

When searching through PD Advantage, it clearly shows most diary keepers write down the *dial position* more than slogans, format or call letters **combined**. This may be because Arbitron encourages precision when writing down dial positions in the diaries. Why go against the grain. If your audience finds it easy to remember you that way, brand yourself in that manner so they'll *write down* your station.

The one thing other stations in your market cannot duplicate are your **personalities!**

The stronger your talent, the stronger your brand. Powerful personalities with great shows provide a unique experience for the listener, therefore generating more TSL and a greater opportunity to be *written down!*

CHAPTER SIXTEEN
IF I WANTED TO BE A 'SURFER,' I'D BUY A BOARD.
How too-many choices have made radio listening difficult.

The object of all marketing is to be persuasive. To move your listeners to think, feel or do something. Building a **brand** involves elements of persuasion and integrity. We're asked to deal with unprecedented change in our media world (satellite radio, HD, I-Pods, internet radio, etc). We cut paths through too-much uncharted territory, as Captain Kirk would say, at 'warp-speed.'

So granted, we do too much with much less time,. Multitasking has become a way of life for most of us. The real problem plaguing radio today is the amount of choices the listener has. It's become a confusing proposition to **listen** to the radio! We have always felt as a society that choice is good and choice is related to freedom, which is essential to our well-being. The more choices we have, the more freedom we have, the better off we are.

It doesn't occur to anyone to question or challenge that statement and is pretty much a no-brainer. Two is better than 1 and three is better than two. Problem is **now** we're talking about 25-30 radio stations in a market, not to mention all other media options. What was once a *liberating* experience is now *paralyzing* our ability to make a simple decision. We've become a nation of "**surfers**" instead of **"consumers."**

In the age of radio consolidation, this has become an even more pressing problem. We're not persuading listeners to stay with us long-enough to enjoy their experience. A listener may hear what they perceive to be a **great song**, only to start surfing the dial with the thought that there's an even **better** song they're missing! In reality, this becomes a self-fulfilling prophesy. Good is never *good-enough.* We're chasing our tail to spite our face.

Listeners *pay* for our service with their time spent listening. Yet, the inability to decide and stay with one particular station is there even when money isn't at stake. As choices increase, listeners actually have a more difficult time finding what they really like. When you're *surfing* you're not *consuming,* therefore, you're never fully satisfied with your experience.

At Sound Advantage Media, I've developed a method of increasing TSL and listener loyalty that cuts through the clutter and gives your audience ownership with their favorite radio station. Here are a few examples:

Stay Topical & Local.
Find out what interests your listeners. What are their hobbies? What are their "hot" buttons? Where do they enjoy "hanging-out?" If you don't know, *find out!* You'd be surprised how your TSL will increase once you've addressed what interests them.

Is Your Programming Relevant To Your Audience?
Not only do you need to be *topical & local,* make sure what you do on-air is relevant to what the audience is searching for! A good way to accomplish this is to have a staff member go through your local newspaper and cut-out two weeks' worth of letters-to-the-editor. This is an inexpensive way to research your listeners "**hot buttons.**"

Is Your Imaging Local?

Focus the imaging of your station on local items of interest to your audience. This gives you some intimacy with the listener and show's you're in-tune with the issues of your community. Great opportunity to become relatable while pushing their **'hot-buttons."** Have local community leaders and P1 listeners record your imaging. People "love" to hear themselves on the radio. This will make you **stand out** in a very crowded marketplace while branding you as your community's radio station.

Involve Your Audience.

Become a two-way communications center for your listeners. Not just for contests and games! People become more attached and loyal to a station they have a personal involvement in. By branding your station as *"My Country 105,"* or *"My Oldies 106 WOLL,"* you've embraced the listener on a much more emotional level. People will take ownership of your station when they have a reason to do so. Increased cume and TSL will follow. People purchase items based on an emotional response. It stands to reason they'll listen to your radio station for the same reason.

No amount of marketing or advertising can save a bad radio station. You need to get your **"act"** together before

Branding your product. People are more cynical today, and the Internet makes it too easy to listen elsewhere.

Radio has forgotten that it's a part of "show-business." You must offer the **"act"** that's unique in the marketplace in order to survive. Anything that makes your listener grateful for your engaging, entertaining,

Stimulating radio station means they are more likely to pass it on! Everyone likes to be the one to share something interesting with their circle of friends. It's up to *you* to give them something to share.

CHAPTER SEVENTEEN
STRONG RADIO STATION POSITIONERS

Strong positioners move a radio station past utility grade. Nearly all of the listening going on in the United States is utility not foreground, not a reason for listening. It's about getting your radio station near the useful part of the curve. That means moving away from being a utility.

Utilities by nature get taken for granted. Radio by its nature also gets taken for granted. You turn on the Country station to hear Country. Classic Hits to hear Classic Hits, etc. That's not all bad but that's not all there can be! If you're just a utility you have no top-of-mind awareness and are very easily replaced. Consider how to be more!

You need to break through the utility status and become something that transfers to an emotional level. Beyond just awareness. That's your opportunity, where the great radio stations have been and will be in the future. If you don't believe you're a utility think about what you do on-the-air and when your phone calls come in. You receive the calls when you don't do what you're expected to do. Miss a school closing or traffic report and see what happens!

The golden opportunity in positioning is to build high profile, difficult to duplicate, desirable attributes that break through the utility status. Easy to accomplish? NO.

Mass Appeal Attributes.

What's difficult to duplicate? Great Air Personalities! That's true for every station. Put something on the air that's entertaining and listeners can't get anywhere else and watch your AQH change dramatically. Powerful positioners include non-musical positive differentiation and a robust sense of character. You need to ask yourself; what are the character words that describe my radio station? If you're going to be high-profile, you need to take a risk.

Principals of Defense.

Defense must be played by a leader. The way to play defense is to attack your own weakness. A great radio station that's on top ratings and revenue wise wants to stay there and is scared all-the-time. The radio station management thinks, "What can they do to me?" "Where am I venerable?" How would you attack your OWN radio station? What would you do about it? Do it NOW!

Defense is about never letting a product attribute be introduced that you think has ANY POTENTIAL without covering your base! This means: Don't wait and see! If you like it, cover it... seem obvious? Confusion *always* benefits the leader! You never attack strength, you attack weakness. Continuously play offense. Figure out the competitions weakness and a way that's too uncomfortable for them to cover!

Flanking.

Flanking is a wonderful attack method. Move into an uncontested area. Becoming the first Country or Classic Hits station in your market, etc. If you flank, surprise is everything. Pursuit is the whole shebang. You cannot just be listener focused; you have to be competitively aware. Country accomplished this by flanking the young demo, positive differentiation, unique selling proposition, relative advantage, "Not your Parents Country Station."

A single relative advantage may come from a single point of differentiation —"Your Hometown Station," "Country's Hottest Hits," "Pure Rock n Roll," etc. Don't allow a complex cluster of values such as service, strong personalities, sports, entertainment, take you down. If you're amused, chances are someone else will be also. Keep the creativity! Don't get anal. Doesn't matter how you get there, as long as the journey is worth it in the long run.

CHAPTER EIGHTEEN
KEEP YOUR RADIO STATION IMAGING FRESH

Radio station imaging is defined as audio recordings played to promote the station. Other terms for imaging have included sweepers, promos, ids, liners and station ids.

Anything not well preserved will at some point be reduced to destruction. The same is true for radio stations. Occasionally when a Program Director loves their imaging, the inclination is, he or she doesn't take the time to change it. You need to keep your message fresh and relevant to your listeners at all times.

It's critical to create an imaging time-table. Chart out a specific theme or idea for the entire year's imaging. January can be used as a New Year subject, Valentine's for February, March for spring, etc.

Remember to always be consistent with your station's slogan. It's critical that you possess a universal slogan that sticks to the station's brand. Some examples include:" ------ you're #1 Hit Music Station" or" Easy Going Favorites" for a Lite Rock station. When using catchphrases and teasers, they should not be confused with slogans! Slogans are permanent as long as the station's format does not change. Teasers are just mini-slogans that tie up the present imaging, promos, events and personality liners altogether. Teasers may change.

Become unique!

Very often, the only line not blurred between competing stations is their call letters. Your station must stand out in a competitive marketplace. Think outside the box and don't be afraid to break some rules. The only feedback to see if you're imaging works is your listeners. Pay attention to what they say. Ask them what they want to hear and what they need to hear. Probe into their lifestyle and incorporate that into your imaging.

One adage of today's marketing is radio listeners react to testimonials. Nonetheless, sometimes listeners don't sound "genuine." Would a real person actually say? "...lots of FUN in the morning and the most music all day." "...makes me want to dance." Before placing testimonials on the air, ask yourself "does this sound real." Creative and realistic imaging becomes an important part of your stations character regardless of the audience measuring apparatus. Always keep the message clear and avoid clutter at all costs. Fresh imaging will enhance your product and serve a purpose for both the station and listener.

CHAPTER NINETEEN
I LEARNED ABOUT PROGRAMMING RADIO STATIONS IN GRADE SCHOOL

There were some important lessons learned when I was in grade school that are just as important now as they were back in the-day. In no particular order of importance, here they are:

• Do your homework (research) and play songs your listeners love. Steer clear of songs they don't love. Play those songs in great repetition.

• Have a conversation with your listeners in the same approach friends use when they're talking with friends, not like strangers.

• If you show you truly enjoy being with your listeners, they'll enjoy being with you as well.

• Similar to when you were a child, don't force your listeners to eat all their vegetables all the time. From time to time, throw them some candy.

• Provide your listeners presents while throwing a party for them, inviting all their friends. This makes them feel special and wanted.

• Turn your listener's favorite music into a diversion that's fun to play which they can share with their friends.

• If you must communicate bad news to your listeners, mentally hold their hand, telling them how sorry you are. Let them express sorrow if they need to.

• Give your listeners a gift for no particular reason. You'll surprise them and maybe they'll tell a friend.

• Don't discuss things your listeners are not aware of. You'll make them feel as if they're a stranger. Remember to include them in everything. Everyone wants to belong.

• Keep in mind the ordinary and mundane toys are not the ones they'll rush over to play with. Search for the unusual, intriguing, and fascinating toys.

• Listeners will always become interested in pictures you take and post on your website if they are in them.

• Cookies and milk are satisfying and good for you. Give your listeners some special treats.

• If you select a special place your listeners have never been, surround them with things that are familiar to make them feel safe and comfortable. Never leave them alone.

• If you want your listeners to remember something, be special and put it to song. It's how we learned our A-B-Cs.

• You still remember the kids in grade school which you cherished and you remember the ones you hated. The kids you were indifferent around have disappeared from your life. Don't allow your radio station to be indifferent to your listeners.

• Leave items on your radio station where your listeners can find them. Traffic, news, weather, sports, great music and their favorite personalities.

• You anticipated your teachers would teach math, spelling, social studies, English, etc. The ones you fondly remember did something extra in your life. Your stations listeners expect great music while keeping them updated on news, traffic and weather. What's that something further you can do that will delight your listeners?

• Don't squander your listener's time with things they don't enjoy. Get to the point, make your break brief, and then return rapidly to the reason they listen to you.

• Become attentive in removing the bad items from your station and replacing it with good.

• Discuss with your listeners things they are interested in. Don't talk about the substance they're not interested in.

• Try and take a nap every day. Wake up with a fresh viewpoint of your station.

• Once you're out into the world, look out for traffic, hold hands, and above all, stick together. It takes teamwork to make a radio station successful. Success is a team sport! You can't obtain ratings by focusing on the ratings. You get ratings by creating a great radio station listeners love!

• Live a well-adjusted life. Make sure you learn and think and play and pray while working every day. Certainly your listener's life isn't just about radio. Yours should not be, either.

CHAPTER TWENTY
RADIO LISTENERS MOST FREQUENT COMPLAINTS

COMMERCIALS

For the most part, they sound terrible!

The pure unending nature of stop sets.

No matter how great the rest of a station's programming may be, most stations are running 16 units or more per hour usually in two breaks.

This makes them unlistenable.

Audiences have complained about commercials for a long time but in a world where listeners can skip commercials everywhere else, radio is looking for real trouble by running unending stop sets.

CBS loads clusters with garbage. Cumulus and Clear Channel throw anything in of any length that they can sell or giveaway to make the listening experience that much worse.

Miller Kaplan Arase has performed more damage to an already bad situation than even PPM could do, as owners want to drive the revenue numbers up at the expense of what is unimaginable to sit through.

The good news is that there are new ways to approach the need to run lots of inventory without driving listeners away. It's a phased plan. You can even test it until you're satisfied.

REPETITIVE MUSIC

An old complaint made worse by the fact that listeners now have many devices to turn to besides radio.

A music radio station operates under the assumption that if they can get a listener to like a song, the listener will stay tuned in for all of it.

There is new evidence that this is no longer possible and changes would be prudent for stations looking to keep audiences engaged.

There is a way to capture even more TSL with music radio listeners by doing something very disruptive – but you're going to like it and you can experiment in off-hours until you feel really confident.

To do nothing will bring more of the same declining time spent listening to radio, while your listeners are listening to something else.

ANTIQUATED MORNING SHOWS

Radio stations are essentially doing the same morning show they've done for 40 years or more. Not one major new element has been innovated and many of the tried and true morning show features that we as an industry love are no longer working.

We're going to brainstorm together about new features to add to morning shows that are unique, compelling and even more importantly, addicting. Take them home and try them. Better yet, try them and sell them. Make them advertiser friendly.

CONTESTS AND PROMOTIONS

They think most radio contests are stupid and the prizes are laughable yet in an era where gaming is so popular, radio has an opportunity to lead the way with contests and promotions so strong that even young listeners will feel compelled to stay glued to the radio. Increasing cume and TSL.

This would be just talk if we didn't have a great promotion that should be done in every market. If you like it, reserve it for yours. The one thing today's listeners expect from a radio contest – even more important than the size of the prize.

HYPE

Even if a station does everything else right, hype and self-promotion will backfire. That wasn't always the case. Radio excelled at self-promotion in earlier decades but now there is something more desirable that listeners crave in the digital age.

It is authenticity!

But being authentic is tougher than it sounds especially when you're transforming the entire radio station.

And there are 6 other things that millennial listeners want from radio in addition to authenticity. Let's go through them one at a time.

The good news is that radio operators who care about local audiences can do something to change audience perceptions.

You just have to know what works and what doesn't.

What to say and what not to.

What to do that excites.

Here are some examples:

1. Disrupting what consolidators have turned our radio industry into.

We can't do this by just changing formats. It's going to take a nuclear option and I've got one for you that is so big it will push your consolidated competitors back with no option to compete with you.

2. Master digital.

Digital isn't a product. It's a technology. Every radio broadcaster needs to start a second stream of revenue separate from radio. Let's create some content. There are some amazing possibilities out there.

3. Create your own social media.

If you tie yourself to Facebook, Twitter or even the current rage, Instagram, you're going down with them. There's a better way. Make your own social network and drive it with content and revenue possibilities. It's being done under the radar by some smart radio people right now.

4. Reinvent radio.

Stop thinking of it as hourly hot clocks and redesign it to be compelling to the very audience we can't seem to attract – 95 million Millennials. They dislike radio but they like some things we're not currently doing. Interested in providing this content for younger money demos? It takes an open mind and some creativity.

5. Video. Video.

Video. We're wasting valuable time. You must be in this business but it is not what you think it is. Let me share some real success stories including one entrepreneur who makes $3 million a year by doing a free 5-minute weekly video. No commercials, banner ads, product placement or subscription fees.

6. The key to attracting Millennials.

There is basically nothing radio has to offer right now that Millennials can't get somewhere else. The secret to attracting Millennials is to build your station for them. I know that sounds awful, but Steve Jobs didn't design Apple products for later adopters. He mastered the early adopters by finding out the "radical" things they couldn't resist. We can do this and here's the plan.

7. Time shift radio.

Look, if you get nothing else out of this you must become skilled at time shifting content. Binge watching is the rage. Broadcasting is out. It doesn't mean the end if we know how to time shift our content.

CHAPTER TWENTY-ONE
WEEKEND PROGRAMMING

Every Friday afternoon is the same everywhere. Your audience, plowing along on that dismal highway of life, spots an off ramp and for two days takes a detour. Their mindset changes along with their pace. Their priorities change. And as a radio station, you need to reflect that or appear hopelessly out of touch with the ambiance of the audience.

A quick reminder: "Ambiance" is the byproduct, the plutonium so-to-speak when you combine Attitude and Emotion. Great radio stations have ambiance.

I've always loved weekend contesting and themes because they allow listeners to divert from whatever they've been doing all week and be topical. Great weekends in Radio are all about being topical and addressing what everyone is murmuring about.

"Great" radio stations "get" so many things, including weekend themes. They understand that starting at 5 on Friday, ambiance =prize. You can take pretty much any prize, any download, any ticket, and massage it to fit what the listener is all about.

So when Pamela reaches out to me on a Wednesday and says "I have Katy Perry tickets this weekend, what should we do?" the first thing I would ask is: What's trending with the Rihanna listeners right now?

It could be Labor Day, back to school, oppressive heat. Possibly a sports scandal. Maybe a celebrity wedding. Or a Disney cruise for you and the entire family!

Other good theme starters? Begin with the name of the prize. Imagine Dragons tickets morphed into imaging gone by a "power of positive thinking shrink" encouraging the audience to visualize, to imagine their tickets. Realization comes from visualization. Substance such as that. They also threw in some Medieval Times tickets so that the winners could see other imaginary dragons. A Free Ticket Weekend would have been just as exciting.

So if you don't have live talent in your city on the weekend, don't get caught up in the mindset of "We have to give stuff to people for them to like us." No." You just need to have some fun and relevant imaging and sound like the lifestyle of the listeners. Now THAT is a great weekend.

Another great opportunity to add spice and personality to your weekend is with Syndicated Programming. Besides enhancing your station with a national personality that you wouldn't be able to hear otherwise, it creates a chance to steer away from the tight playlists airing on most stations all week. It is also a specialty program and thus your sales department can sell it as such and create revenue not otherwise realized by the station. A win-win for the programming and sales departments.

Let's take a look at what's available in the syndication marketplace. The list is just too long to be complete, so I'll just highlight some of the more popular programs available for weekend programming.

Premiere Networks is the largest syndicator of radio programs in the country. They cover every conceivable format in all available dayparts. Here are some of their most popular music formatted shows: "American Top 40 with Ryan Seacrest." It's a 4 hour program available 6:00am-12:00am local time. The most popular top-40 music with America's longest running weekend countdown and a truly engaging host makes this show a listener favorite on Hot AC and CHR stations.

"Saturday Night Online Live with Romeo" is a uniquely interactive radio show hosted by radio veteran Tim 'Romeo" Herbster. His show reaches listeners across multiple platforms—on-air, online and via social media—creating a complete experience that connects listeners, stars, and advertisers in a bang out Saturday Night party.

Superadio Network also has a wide variety of product available for weekends. They produce three country shows, two Latino shows (plus imaging and spot production), Nine Urban/Rhythmic shows, and two Hot AC shows. The most popular being "Retro Pop Reunion" hosted by Hot AC Talent Joe Cortese. It brings together the biggest hits of the video music era. The show is 2 hours long and airs either Saturday or Sunday 6AM-8PM local time.

United Stations Radio Network runs Radio Hall of Famer personality Dick Bartley. He hosts three separate shows on weekends, for Oldies or Classic Hits formatted radio stations. He's been hosting America's Classic Hits request radio show since 1982. Debuting as "Solid Gold Saturday Night," the program has been known as "Rock & Roll's Greatest Hits!" since 1991.

A weekly, four-hour countdown show presented in a fast passed, Top 40 style, "The Classic Countdown" features exclusive interview comments from the musicians, songwriters and producers who made the music. Bartley also hosts the "Sunday Night Countdown" on New York's legendary WCBS-FM 101.1 which streams on wcbsfm.com every Sunday evening 8PM to Midnight Eastern time.

Another busy guy is WCBS-FM Morning Man Scott Shannon. He has a syndicated four-hour Classic Hits formatted show titled: "America's Greatest Hits." It currently runs on ten CBS Classic Hits stations plus additional affiliates and is syndicated by United Stations Radio Network.

There are literally hundreds of syndicated shows to fit any format that will increase ratings and ROI. This partial list has just scratched the surface of the product available. Take my advice; pick up one or two of these or other shows for YOUR station. You'll be surprised how well they'll sound and how much money you will make selling advertising time!

CHAPTER TWENTY-TWO
MOST RADIO STATIONS HAVE BAD WEBSITES

Are you like me? Do you surf to your local radio station website only to find yourself asking the question: Why on Earth did I bother to come here?

As a test, and to make sure I wasn't limiting my critique to those stations in markets which have resources of less than zero, I toured the list of station websites in California. I'm told there's lots of ad revenue there, and that means lots of investment in the digital platform, right?

I was only kidding myself.

Here are the things I dislike about radio station websites, thanks to the arbitrary sampling of California station sites:

1. Site takeovers. If I want to visit your advertiser's website, I'll go there directly without stopping at your landing page version first. Ask the question: Would Coke do this? Would Sears? No. They don't need to. You do it for them.

2. Weather forecasts at the top of the website. I have an app for that, thank you.

3. Invitations to listener clubs with no benefits clarified. The last time I joined a club that had no benefits…um, wait. That never happened.

4. Multiple thumbnail ads on the home page – all of which are the same. I know repetition is important in advertising – but on the same page at the same time?

5. Millions Of items to click on suggesting that the phrase "user experience" must be from some lost civilization.

6. Blogs that don't enable comments

7. Blogs which enable comments but have nobody, strongly suggesting there's nothing there worth commenting on.

8. An obsession with sharing, but no preoccupation with content worth sharing.

9. "Sharing? Why do that? Let's just prostitute Facebook and Twitter."

10. Tiny pictures with tiny text. The trend in online is about LARGER pictures and LARGER text.

11. Sites that look like crap on mobile devices, implying that nobody at the station has ever tried to view their own site on one.

12. Little or no attention given to podcasts, or podcasts which are more difficult to find than Jimmy Hoffa's remains.

13. Podcasts which work fine on PC's – which are rapidly vanishing – but not at all on mobile devices – the things that are replacing PC's.

14. Online streams which are more than one easy click away. Worse than that, NO streaming at all!

15. Streams which are preceded by the tiny message: "Streaming is limited to listeners in California," thus defeating the purpose of a platform which, last time I checked, was global.

16. Any pictures of Katy Perry. Especially if they're on multiple station sites at the same time.

17. Logo banners where the logo is on the right instead of the left – oops, sorry, there is no such thing. I might as well believe in Santa Clause. All logos go on the left. It states that in the Geocities design manual.

10. Logo banners showing a bunch of stock photo artist images, because nothing says your station is different like the same artists everyone else has on their logo banners.

19. A page so cluttered with ads it makes one crave for the editorial style of the Pennysaver

20. A solicitation to download the mobile app. I'm sorry; I didn't see any of those.

21. No way to personalize the experience of your brand, therefore no reason to sign in (like I do to virtually every online destination that matters to me).

CHAPTER TWENTY-THREE
TEN RULES FOR SUCCESSFUL RADIO

1) <u>DESIRE</u>:

A radio station must **want** to win, and have the intense desire to create something very special. Listeners can perceive that burning desire to be good at what we do.

2) <u>CONSISTENCY:</u>

The number one enemy of success is not sticking with **The Plan**, worse yet, not having a plan at all. Establish a game plan and stick to it! Inconsistency is frequent changes caused by:

- **Impatience**
- **Boredom**
- **Lack of commitment**
- **Lack of confidence**
- **Desire to be different**
- **Distractions**

Successful radio **today** is not always produced overnight.

3) <u>SIMPLICITY:</u>

Great stations are simple stations. We **never** confuse the listener. This means, **play the right songs!** On a music station 70% or more of any hour is music, but often little or no investment is made to ensure the station is playing the right songs. How do wrong songs happen? A number of reasons:

- **Assumptive familiarity**
- **Lack of research**
- **PD or MD personal favorite**
- **Right Songs; Wrong Order**
- **The PD or GM's spouse likes it**
- **To get the trip/concert/promotion**
- **Lost causes—outdated bands and songs we "wish" we could still play**
- **"We got a request for it"**

4) <u>KNOW THE MARKET:</u>

Do you and your staff really know and understand who your target audience really is, and what their needs are? Successful stations use a variety of research tools to better understand their market, competition, listeners, strengths and weaknesses. Research allows you to benchmark your progress and determine if you are cutting through, and how your target audience perceives your programming. This includes:

- **Perceptual Research**—Market, Lifegroup, Cume, Group/Cluster
- **Music Research**—Library (Auditorium), Currents (Callout), On-Line
- **Arbitron**—PD Advantage, Maximi$er, Scarborough, Trending
- **One-On-One**—Focus Groups, Listener Panels
- **Research on A Budget**—Listener Panels, Internet Surveys/Polls, Internet Music Tests, Waiters & Waitresses

5) BE LOCAL:

Great radio stations know one of the ways to winning is super serving their community. Having staff and air talent who live, love and play in your community is critical. Be tapped into what's going in your community, then deliver this information in a useable and interesting form to your target audience.

6). PROTECT THE PRODUCT:

Successful stations have an acutely strong vision of what the station should sound like and they protect the product at all costs. They protect:

- **Listener Expectations**
- **Against Clutter**
- **Promotions**
- **Music Credibility**
- **Consistency**
- **Against Conflicting Agendas**

7) BUILDING PRODUCT LOYALITY:

One that great product is in place you can increase cume by building product loyalty. Successful stations understand the importance of P1 listeners and have a "personal relationship" with them. P1's are your "Best Customers". They are the 36% of your audience giving you 72% of your quarter hours. Giving your P1's the **special attention** they deserve is achieved through a variety of methods:

- **Features and Special Programming**
- **Listener/Membership Club**
- **Newsletter/Mailings**
- **Email**
- **Website**
- **Communication/Input**
- **Preferred Concert Seating/Tickets**
- **Birthday Cards**

- **Private Concerts**
- **CD Samplers**
- **Polls/Surveys**

8) <u>ADVANCE PLANNING:</u>

Successful stations plan well in-advance so the most important—not necessarily the most urgent—strategies are executed first. The **most** positive results of Advance Planning are:

- **Station Needs Come First**
- **Less Clutter**
- **Less Stress**
- **Better Communication**
- **Better Execution**

Some of the basic tools successful stations use to plan include:

- **12 Month Calendar**
- **Arbitron Overlay**
- **Holiday and Recurring Event Overlay**
- **Promo Inventory Management**

9) <u>GETTING CREDIT:</u>

Too many radio stations miss a great opportunity to get tics in an Arbitron survey diary for all the great things they do on and off the air. After all, we are also in the diary influencing business! Simply attaching your name to all contests, features and events will make a **huge** difference, providing it's done well with good production values, a good voice and hopefully some clever copy. Your brand needs to be on the top of mind both on air and in your market. Get your logo at all the places your listeners frequent.

10) <u>GOOD ENVIRONMENT:</u>

Successful stations are professional, forward-thinking organizations that hire and train the best people, and keep them happy. They have great chemistry. It's much more difficult to find great staff in the new millennium. As we all know it's not always about the money,.....it's benefits, the work environment, and the level of fun that all lead to job satisfaction. This is the key to retaining a great staff, so when someone offers them a job they are less likely to even consider it. When your station creates staff loyalty it makes it difficult for existing or new competitors to come after you. A loyal staff that works together as a team doesn't just happen! It takes **leadership!** Once the team is in place, motivation, inspiration and gratitude naturally follow. This is best achieved through:

- **Training Well**
- **Offering Incentives/Bonuses**
- **Involvement**
- **Holding Them Accountable**

CHAPTER TWENTY-FOUR
RADIO CONSULTANT-STATION MANAGEMENT
RELATIONSHIP

When the discussion is on value and the radio station is convinced of the wisdom of a relationship with you, fees become academic. (It's always amazed me that realtors, for example, casually accept a 6% standard commission, when no laws or regulations prohibit a higher commission in return for a higher level of service.) Here are some approaches to develop strong relationships that demonstrate value and result in much higher commitment from the client, and resultant higher consulting fees:

1. Find out what the radio station's objectives are, personally and professionally. These elements are always intertwined in the sale or acquisition of a station or group. People think based on logic, but they act based on emotion. Find out what visceral needs the client holds dearest, and demonstrate how they will be met, safeguarded, or otherwise supported.

2. Suggest additional outcomes for the client. Every client I've ever met knows what he or she wants, but few know what they need. The difference between want and true need is you're value-added. Once a prospect says, "I've never looked at it that way before," you have a high quality relationship created.

3. Focus on output, not input. No one cares about your advertising or offices. People don't buy drills because they love the tool; they buy because they need holes. Demonstrate important outcomes for the client, such as speed, promotions, higher ROI, increased ratings, branding opportunities and changeover management. The only real test is when the business changes hands on terms that are beneficial to me and meet or exceed my objectives.

4. Provide assurances and guarantees. Supply testimonials, endorsements and references that are tightly analogous to the particular prospect's position. Allow others to sing your praises. Two people swearing that you were instrumental to their success beat's a $1,000 brochure any day of the week.

5. Listen, listen, and listen. I'm buying a new car, and price is no object. Yet most of the sales people insist on delivering a pitch, telling me how to drive, or suggesting features that don't interest me. You can't learn while you're talking. Develop some provocative questions and follow up questions, and keep the prospect talking until you have enough emotional and factual information to embrace them as partners. Don't teach your sales people "closing techniques" or "features and benefits" spiels. Teach those questioning skills and relationship building techniques. This has been accomplished with sales people all over the country.

One more item: Everyone in your office from secretary to sales person to accountant has a role in client relationships. I've taken my business away from otherwise solid professionals whose office staff was rude, incompetent, or unfriendly. Clients want their phone calls returned promptly, and 24 hours is not prompt (my own standard is 90 minutes which I hit 99% of the time, and my clients are amazed).

Stop developing marketing campaigns and start developing relationships. Both the top line--sales--and the bottom line--margin-- will improve dramatically, and it doesn't get much better than that.

CHAPTER TWENTY-FIVE
ARE YOU LISTENING?

It amazes me as I travel as a Radio Consultant, how many people **don't** listen! We don't listen to our audience, our advertisers or our colleagues. As an industry and a society, we need to hear what people are really saying. Listening is one of the most important abilities you can possess. How well you listen has a direct influence on your job efficiency, as well as the quality of your relationships with others.

- We listen to acquire information
- We listen to comprehend
- We listen for enjoyment
- We listen to gain knowledge

You'd think with all the listening we're supposed to be doing; we'd be good at it!

Recent research suggests we only remember between 25 to 50 percent of what we actually hear. That means when you speak to your boss, listeners, colleagues or spouse for 10 minutes, they're paying attention to less than half of the conversation. This is miserable!

If you turn that around it reveals when you are being presented with information or receiving directions, you are not hearing the entire message either. You can only anticipate the important parts are captured in your 25-50 percent, but what if they're not?

Obviously, listening is a skill we can all benefit from improving upon. By becoming an improved listener, you'll increase your productivity, as well as your ability to influence, persuade and negotiate. Furthermore, you will avoid conflict and misunderstandings. All of which are essential for career achievement!

A good communication ability needs a strong level of self-awareness. By understanding your personal type of communicating, you will go much further creating lasting impressions with others. The way to become a better listener is to practice "dynamic listening." This is when you make a conscious attempt to hear not only the words but understanding the whole message being sent.

Don't become too distracted by everything else around you, or by forming counter arguments in your head when the other person stops speaking. You can't get bored by losing focus on what the other person is saying. This will contribute to poor listening and understanding.

To improve your listening abilities, you need to acknowledge to the other person you're listening to what's being said. To understand the importance of this action, ask yourself if you've ever been involved in a conversation when you wondered if the other person was listening at all. Is your message coming across, or is it worthwhile continuing to speak. You want to avoid the feeling as if you're speaking to a brick wall.

Acknowledgement is as easy as a simple nod of the head. You don't have to show agreement, just an indication that you're listening. Body language will acknowledge you are listening while keeping your attention on the conversation and not let you mind wonder.

Respond to the speaker in a way that will both encourage him or her to continue speaking, so you may receive all the information that you need. While nodding show's you're interested, a sporadic question or comment to recap what has been said communicates you understand the message as well.

Here are five fundamentals of dynamic listening:

1. Pay Attention
Give the speaker your undivided attention, and acknowledge the message. Realize that non-verbal communication "speaks" loudly.

- Observe the speaker directly
- Place distracting thoughts aside
- Don't mentally prepare a rebuttal!
- Stay away from environmental elements. For example, side conversations.

2. Indicate you're listening
Practice your own body language to convey your attention.

- Occasionally nod
- Use facial expressions like smiling
- Make sure your posture is open and attractive
- Inspire the speaker with small verbal comments like yes or no

3. Encourage Feedback
Personal filters, assumptions, judgments, and beliefs will distort what we hear. As a listener, you must understand what's being said. This could require some reflection and ask questions.

- Reflect what's been said by paraphrasing, "What I'm hearing is," and "Sounds like you are saying." This is a terrific reflection tool.
- Ask questions that will clarify certain aspects of the conversation. "What do you mean when you say," "Is this what you mean?"
- Periodically summarize the speaker's comments.

4. Postpone Judgment

Interrupting is nothing more than a waste of time. It will frustrate the speaker and limits full understanding of the message.

- Permit the speaker to finish before asking questions
- Don't interrupt with counter arguments

5. React Appropriately

Dynamic listening is a representation for respect and understanding. You're accumulating information and perspective. Nothing is enhanced by attacking the speaker or putting him or her down.

- Be candid, open and honest when you respond
- Support your opinions with respect
- Handle the other person the way you would like to be treated

There's a lot of concentration and willpower to become a dynamic listener. There are a lot of old habits to overcome and they're tough to break. If you're listening habits are as terrible as most people, there's a lot of old habit-breaking to perform. Keep reminding yourself that the goal is to hear what the other person is saying. Concentrate on the message by setting aside other thoughts and behaviors. Ask questions, reflect and paraphrase to guarantee you understand the message. Begin using dynamic listening immediately and you will become a much better communicator, improve workplace productivity, and acquire better personal relationships.

CHAPTER TWENTY-SIX
MARRY YOUR LISTENERS!
Build a winning franchise and increase TSL in your market.

Radio is an art form but also a business. Producing great radio involves both commerce and art. But more than art & business, successful radio stations are **married to their listeners.** When we fail to satisfy our listener's needs and desires, we don't meet listener expectations or revenue goals. As an industry we need to rejuvenate the creative spark in our radio product. Radio's underlying sameness from market to market has created a homogenization in sound across the country. Our creativity has been stifled in the name of corporate profit. This is a problem, especially in small to medium markets.

In my 30 years experience as a Program Director and Air Personality in Large, Medium and Small markets across the country, and now as a consultant, I've seen great radio stations succeed because they foster a strong creative environment coupled with strong leaders who act as mentors. Station employees who tap into that well of creativity and apply it to their everyday craft, help build winning franchises. Radio works best when it connects emotionally with its listeners; just like good marriages. And satisfied listeners are good customers.

Here are a few examples of building that winning franchise and increasing TSL in **your** market:

BE LOCAL!

The more locally focused your presentation, the greater the opportunity to serve your community with excellence. **"Local" should become your new buzzword**. Great stations know one of the best ways to winning an audience is having an air staff that live, love, and play in the community. Become tapped into what's going on in your town or city, and then deliver the information in a useable and interesting form to your listeners. Communicate!

KNOW THE MARKET!

Chain stations are programmed from far away and while everyone likes the "hits", not every market has the same interests, hobbies, spare-time activities, etc. Do you and your staff understand what your target audience interests are? Do you understand their needs and wants? Are you **listening** to your audience or are you **vulnerable** to attack from the competition? If you don't know the answers to those questions, you **are** vulnerable.

"Ask yourself, as if you were the competition: "where are they the weakest? " Fix that area ASAP. Use research to benchmark your progress and determine if you're cutting through the clutter, and how your target audience perceives your programming

PUT YOUR WEBSITE TO WORK

If you don't have a web site; for shame, get one! Maintain a site where listeners can answer surveys and take part in special on-line-only contests. Make it **fun** and involve the listener often, at least twice per day part. And remember, **stream, stream, stream** your audio. This will allow you to pick up listeners in un-conventional ways. Do you really care **where** their listening as long as they're listening? Go where your listeners are going. Today that often means the internet.

KISS (Keep It Simple…)

Great stations are **simple** stations. We **never** confuse the listener. This means not just **playing the right songs**, but **playing them in the right order** and giving your play list some expansion. On music stations, 70% or more of any given hour is music. Make sure your air staff's comments reflect the music and image of your station.

CONSISTENCY

More than just needing to be **simple**, we need to be **consistent** and stick with a well thought out game plan. Worse than not sticking with your plan, is **not** having a plan to begin with. Inconsistency is frequently caused by:

- **Boredom**
- **Impatience**
- **Lack of commitment**
- **Lack of confidence**
- **Too many distractions**

Today's successful stations are not produced overnight.

FAILURE IS NOT AN OPTION!

Don't **fail** your listeners. If you are in a marriage worth saving, you go to counseling to see how to be successful again. Your radio station is no different. How do we often fail?

- **Lack of research**
- **Assumptive familiarity**
- **"Personal Favorite" of the PD or MD**
- **To get the trip/concert/promotion**
- **Rights Songs; Wrong Order**
- **Someone called in a "requested song."**

START MENTORING

The encouragement of a strong creative environment begins with a mentoring program. Successful stations are professional, forward-thinking organizations which hire and train the very best people, and find a way to keep them **happy!** In the new millennium, it's a much more difficult task to find a great air staff and productive sales people. We need to bring "communications" back into the communications industry.

Successful mentoring starts with: **Leadership:** Delegate authority and encourage teamwork. Be different. Don't follow conventional rules blindly. Become passionate about your projects. When management is excited and enthusiastic, a trickledown effect occurs.

Involvement: Don't reject ideas out of hand because they seem wild, crazy, or unproven. People who are involved in a decision making process participate much more enthusiastically than those who just carry out their
Boss's orders. Help them contribute and show them you value their opinions.

Brainstorm: Something normally thought of as a group activity, is also a great area for private problem-solving. Do it **away** from the station. Find a quiet place; a park, someone's home, a friendly restaurant with private meeting rooms; any place where management and staff can feel mentally and physically comfortable to talk.

Incentives/Bonuses: Showing your staff you appreciate their hard work and good ideas with bonuses or incentives helps create staff loyalty, making it difficult for competitors to lure your best people away.

Ford Motor Company claims "Quality is Job #1." We need to think of our radio product in the very same way! Most families have a family physician and dentist, an insurance agent and your favorite hair stylist. Why can't we also have a **family favorite** radio station? **Any** radio station can become wed to its listeners for life. You simply need to communicate with them and the desire to always keep them **happy!**

Congratulations! And may you both be happy and successful together for the rest of your lives.

CHAPTER TWENTY-SEVEN
ARE YOU A NONSTOP BRANDER?
This is what every radio station should accomplish.

Think of rebranding not as an occurrence, but rather a procedure. Rebranding is like shifting tectonic plates. As long as the shifting is a slow nearly imperceptible continuous movement, everything is fine. It is only when the plates freeze up and pressure builds, that shifting becomes violent and damaging. That's the way to think about rebranding. You want the changes to be gradual and continuous. If the radio station goes a long time without an update, it is just like two interior continental plates getting stuck. Sooner or later, something's going to give, and an earthquake erupts.

So the key is to create a continuous rebranding strategy is as follows:

The first thing you need to do is make a list of all the elements that go into creating the station's identity. Think about what makes the station what it is. You will be surprised. Virtually every department plays a role in giving the station its distinctive personality. And you will include every one of them as you inventory what needs to be updated when you rebrand. Here are some starter suggestions:

In programming you've got the music–what you play and what you don't play. Then there are rotations. Rotations, scheduling rules, and flow can have a dramatic impact on how a station sounds even if the library doesn't vary. There's the air staff. Regardless of the quality of your staff and how long they have been on the air, this too needs to change from time to time. There's how much they talk, what they talk about, and how they say it. If you want to change things, move the staff around. Moving people can often have a dramatic effect as replacing people.

Newscasts need to change as more listeners get their headlines from the web. List all the elements of news that need to grow over time. Don't forget special programming and weekend shows. Adding an evening feature, a midday gossip show, or some other special program changes the pace of the station, and provides something new to promote and tease. Every special program should come to an end one day. A show may be doing well, but there's something out there that's even better. Find it and move on. Don't leave engineering out of the list. Changing the over-all texture of the station should be part of the update. Listen critically to the station. Does the station sound contemporary? Think about the processing chain, consider tweaking the EQ, change the mics.

List all the annual promotions (paid and free). Include annual contests, what you give away and how you give it away. Include remotes, both paid and concerts. Contests like special programming should have a sunset date. Inventory the station's marketing. There's the station name and logo. List the logo's elements including things like color, fonts, etc. Change the station's primary positioning statement and liners. Write them all down and list the dates that they were added. Don't forget the station voice. That needs to change at regular intervals. There's the web site and the dozens of elements on the site. There are the station's social media efforts, email. Once you've laid out all the station elements, you'll find that there are dozens of things you should be regularly changing.

The next step is to lay out a rebranding clock. You want to rotate the elements of rebranding as if you're scheduling an hour of music, except instead of an hour, the wheel might be a year or two. If the station is a CHR, then you want to use a fairly fast rotation. If you are an AC, Country, or some other adult format, you'll slow down the rotations. Each month schedule to change something. It might be in marketing one month, programming the next. Schedule changes with sufficient frequency that everything will have changed by the time a year or two rolls around depending on your format. Coordinate with your sister stations so no two stations are changing the same element at the same time. With a group, you'll be able to update and recycle ideas throughout your stations.

A comprehensive list of station elements combined with a schedule of when they need to be updated is the road map for continuous rebranding. It keeps the station fresh, timely, while building audience loyalty and cume.

CHAPTER TWENTY-EIGHT
"BE THE MORALE-BOOSTING GM"

Most of today's best radio managers have literally had to manage people by trial and error. There's no training process for radio management. While it may not be specifically outlined in your duties, you're also overseer of the station's morale. Managing the morale has usually not been one of the main criteria for becoming Program Director or General Manager. Yet, these two positions often dictate the station's management style and the morale that results.

As a consultant, I've noticed the importance of maintaining the staff's confidence as a leader. You can't lead if those following aren't convinced you're the one for the job. You've got to rise above your own personal feelings and let your immediate emotional response pass before you determine how to respond in a conflict.

The basic element in managing and creating positive morale is the art of honest communication. People don't execute what they don't understand. Good communication is a priority of the highest level. People best accomplish that which they embrace, or at the very least understand the importance of.

Taking responsibility for one's actions is another key element in effectively managing people. Owning up to "doing the right thing" at all times is a masterful way to demonstrate integrity while gaining respect of the staff. Whether you caused a problem or not, take the responsibility to bring it to the attention of management so it may be addressed. You have to respect the person who admits to mistakes, asks for help or guidance to correct it, and then does what's necessary to make things work.

How do you best describe your management style? Are you hands-on, laid back, or some place in between? Is it important to "park your ego at the door" in managing people? Each manager has different ways of managing morale. You must hire the best people who can understand and are willing to conform to your standards of excellence. Provide them with the best tools your budget allows. Involve them in all aspects pertaining to department and individual goals, and then establish a system of meetings and reports which allows you to track their progress without interfering with their day-to-day endeavors.

Once a GM or PD has mastered his or her own style, creating a management mission statement for your station or group is an effective way of enlisting your staff and encouraging them to work toward the same goals. Asking them to participate in the process increases morale while creating ownership in the principles important to the collective group.

The ultimate mission statement which I use as a "way of life" is if you believe your station or group is the best place in the state or country to work, ultimately the best people will want to work here.

CHAPTER TWENTY-NINE
AIR PERSONALITY RECIPES

The best radio talent understands how to mix everyday ingredients to create an exceptional recipe. If you're not familiar with Iron Chef America, you should study it. All 4 chefs are given the same five ingredients and an hour to create a masterpiece. The competition is fierce, fast paced and brutal. Welcome to radio.

Think about the content of your show. You have access to the same "show prep" (ingredients) as your competition. The secret to success (recipe) is what you choose to use, how you present it and how much of the secret ingredient you share. That secret ingredient is YOU. No one else can duplicate that one. Here is one "recipe" that I think can help you create a better masterpiece each day.

I am a strong believer in the magic of threes. Let's break the content into three main categories:

Big Dumb Fun	Relationship Engagement	Human Interest
Contesting	Between Spouses	Celebrity interviews
Prank Calls	With parents	Hollywood & Music
War of The Roses	With Friends	News
Telemarketer Calls	Between You & the	Overcoming Obstacles
Parody Songs	Listener	TV Shows
Trivia & Other Games	Co-Workers	Movies
"Are You Kidding Me" News	Community	Books
On & Off-Air Stunts		

The most universally relatable category is RELATIONSHIPS! Everyone has them, most people want them and all of them require nurturing. At least 50% of your ingredients each day should come from that category. Big Dumb Fun is entertaining and can provide much needed laughs. However, the appeal of this category is very subjective and should only comprise 20%. Human interest is necessary so that your listeners are confident that you relevant and up to date on current events. They rely on you to help them feel "in the know". It is the least "unique" of the three categories and therefore only warrants 30% of the mix. All of this must be mixed with YOU as the bonding element.

I put relationships at the center of this recipe because it is the core of what we do. That is where you get the most "bang for your buck" in terms of listener interaction and emotional connection. If you work a music format, the music is all about relationships and provides an easy springboard for topics. Your own relationships and human experiences provide show prep. The possibilities are endless: dating, marriages, raising kids, taking care of aging parents, building a business, etc. Finding hot topics and letting people voice their opinions is extremely powerful.

Once you have the right recipe, think about your presentation. Every 20 minutes there are new people joining the show. You need something new for them to sample that demonstrates your ability to combine all of those ingredients into a perfect and delicious meal that they just can't get enough of. You want them to walk away satisfied but wanting more. Think of yourself as the Iron Chef and accept the challenge of creating a new masterpiece every day.

CHAPTER THIRTY
INTERNET RADIO: IT'S A NICHE WORLD

Internet radio has become more user friendly since its inception in 1994. All you have to do is type one phrase in a search engine and any internet user will reach thousands of distinctive genres of music and radio stations. It truly is mind-boggling and can be more than a bit overwhelming. Car manufacturers such as GM, Ford, and Chrysler have added internet radio to their vehicles. There was a time when car radios cranked out the soundtrack of our lives. That's not the case anymore.

There are several reasons how internet (as well as satellite) radio makes music easily available to any listener.

1. It's simple to locate what you wish to hear fast.
Terrestrial radio requires dial surfing in order to locate what the listener wishes to hear. This can take much more time to find their preference, usually without commercials. With internet radio, the listener is brought to specific links to formats such as Oldies, Classic Rock, Country, Bluegrass as well as a host of others. Not only are there direct links to a sole genre of music but incredible options of multiple stations.

2. A consumer has the ability to listen to custom stations tailored to their preferences.

Pandora, iHeart, Radio Tunes, TuneIn, Live 365 are just a few examples of multiple radio stations popular throughout different demographics around the country. These sites give the listener the ability to specifically create a format around an artist they may particularly like. If the listener disagrees with a song or artist choice, they can simply hit 'thumbs up' or 'thumbs down' and that song, along with others like it, will not appear on the station again. This ability to personalize your favorite internet station to reflect your personal taste is incredibility user-friendly, allowing listeners to create large quantities of custom channels.

3. Music listeners possess diverse tastes and internet radio tailors their specific desires.

Internet radio allows everyone to arrange their own variety of stations tailored how they want. Each user has the ability to discover new artists and genres they may never have found without the internet radio experience. Possessing taste in music is akin to how people desire their food spiced. Sometimes a little is enough and that specific seasoning is provided courtesy of internet radio stations.

The mobile app market is an exploding area of the internet as every internet generating apparatus becomes smaller, sleeker and more user friendly. Internet radio is taking advantage of this mobile app revolution by joining the pact, almost all internet radio stations create app formats that can be downloaded to Apple, Android or Windows phone systems.

Cellular and smartphones which can access the internet are being produced every couple of months. It's a normal routine for every person over twelve to have a phone or tablet on their person at all times. These smart phones can create large databases which stores countless apps with multiple functions. This means there's a large quantity of computer space for developers to utilize. It seems that apps are certainly the future of business whether the business is large or small.

The accessibility of internet radio continues to expand into the world of analog radio. Especially now that smart phones internet apps function anyplace that possesses WiFi. Before this mobility was obtained the internet user was confined to a desktop or laptop computer to listen to custom stations online.

The audio entertainment industry is changing and no one can accurately predict where it's going. One thing is certain; internet radio is having an impact on terrestrial radio broadcasters, and will continue to have an impact as time goes on. Listeners can start their own internet station with little capitol and broadcast anything they want for as long as they want. It's not over-the-air, so the FCC has no jurisdiction regarding content. That's what attracted shock jock Howard Stern to XM/Sirius Satellite Radio. Internet radio has a powerful influence over marketing and new music and is considered by most broadcasting professionals to be more influential than terrestrial radio. The launch of internet radio has paved the way to the new face of advertisement and entertainment.

The internet has brought different successful results to business entrepreneurs. As most of us have begun utilizing the internet, most businessmen have considered it as their conduit to advertise new products and services. It's shown that most business and personal transactions can be performed on the internet, including banking, shopping, and leisure activities.

Meanwhile, Steve Bianchi of Identity Programming in Warwick, RI sees it differently. "For several years, going back to the 90's, the radio, TV and, especially, the newspaper industries were trying to determine how they would react to the onset of internet communications and how it would affect their business. Radio, like the other communication businesses, began to consider the importance of having an outstanding website and extra communication with users and clients though "the net."

However, in too many cases this has caused distraction from improving the actual on air product, coming up with new and unique programming ideas and concentrating on new strategies to combat the onslaught of the various music streaming services. There's a "deer in the headlights" reaction to all of these new offerings on the part of some major radio ownership and management."

The moment you visit a radio website, you'll notice all types of banners of sponsors. This allows for the power of advertisement. Then you choose your type of music or station, this gives the power of entertainment. Having said that; what can be more powerful in creating the impact to any listener? In addition to marketing their own website, internet radio has contracted to promote their own website(s). Not to mention the music industry professionals, everyone who would want to be involved with internet radio in the new millennium.

CHAPTER THIRTY-ONE
BLOG METHODS THAT START A CONVERSATION

The statistics show that only one out of one hundred readers will *ever* comment on your blog. Out of a sample of one hundred, it's common to acquire nine of them who contributes everyone once in a while, another who participates frequently, and ninety who will read the blog without comment. These numbers are not cast in-stone. They will vary from site to site, but the fact remains most people will never leave a blog comment. If you're searching for more comment, here are some suggestions on how to get increased comments on your blog.

1. Request Commentary: When you end the blog, ask for a request to comment. This will prompt people who may be on the fence regarding posting to try their hand at participating in the discussion. Make sure your comment system is simple to use for people tense regarding posting.

2. Invite Queries: Questions always invite an answer. Place a few in your post and you will receive numerous people eager to answer them.

3. Make sure it's Open: Don't make it that you're the master of the conversation. Leave enough room for people to debate and answer your questions with their own take on the situation.

4. Remember to leave Comments on the Comments: This is especially wise for beginning bloggers who don't possess a large following yet. Reply to some of the comments in the comment section. This inspires others to leave comments and show you are listening. Once your blog has grown to a much larger readership, this will not be as simple, but the occasional comment should be made occasionally.

5. Make Sure you Make Rules: One bad poster will make others nervous regarding posting. Create clear guidelines that are set and enforced, this will build an environment which is inviting for commentary.

6. Show some Humility: Readers appreciate it when the blogger displays a measure of humility. It's okay to appear not to be an authority on every subject or that you're human and have made some mistakes along the way. No one wishes to respond to someone who reply's with ignorance or distain.

7. Be Polite: Bloggers are human and are going to make mistakes. There will always be someone who upon reading the blog who will notice this. No mistake will go unseen and people will post about it. That you can be sure of. When you respond, exhibit politeness and tack while you fix the mistake. Acting defensive will only drive people away.

8. Allow some Controversy: This point in and of itself is controversial. Occasionally it doesn't work. There are few occurrences people enjoy commenting upon more than controversy. Just be cautious. Some shy readers of your blog may very well may steer clear at the first hint of controversy and never post.

9. Recognize Comments: Rewarding good or outstanding posts by commenting how good they were is a great tactic. Especially good posts can be mentioned in the main text of the blog. This encourages people with good ideas to make posts of their own.

10. Achieve Easy Commenting: Prevent requiring registration to post comments. This isn't for everyone. Most blogs don't follow this tip. It's another hoop to make bloggers jump through and becomes another barrier to pass for commentary. Numerous readers of your blog may not wish to leave behind personal information or remember another name and password!

CHAPTER THIRTY-TWO
"A TERRIBLE THING HAPPENS WHEN YOU DON'T PROMOTE." NOTHING!

Listeners recycle your radio station an average of every 20 minutes. You always have a fresh audience joining your show. So, you need something original to sample, demonstrating your ability to entertain. Always leave them wanting more.

Define your station before you promote yourself to others. It's called "Positioning." How can we explain to others (promotion) what we do if we aren't clear about it ourselves. Having a focus makes it much easier for the listeners to spread the word about you.

I understand we hate labeling things—it pigeonholes us. But in your audience's ears it helps to define what we do. Besides, it's better to pick a label than let your listeners hang one on you. Is your radio station Blues formatted? Is it Country? Rock? News/Talk? Jazz? AC? Oldies? Maybe a combination of those or something completely different. What else do you do well? Concentrate on your strengths and market those.

Part of promoting your station is knowing what your target audience does on a daily basis. What do they read? Where do they hang out? What websites are they browsing? Do you have a Twitter and Facebook page? Does your station have a website? Does it stream? Knowing an audience means figuring out who they are, what they want, where they are, and how much are they willing to spend!

Promotions are very basic things. You can embellish them as much as you like, **after** the basics are in place. Radio people sometimes find themselves developing full-blown bells-and-whistles-flash-and-dazzle promotions, losing sight of the importance of simple things like first impressions, preparation, knowledge, and good-humor.

You must be visible **everywhere.** You should strive to present a positive image, to establish and nurture relationships, and make each event enjoyable for **everybody,** whether they're faithful listeners (P1's), strangers to the station or format, or the clients themselves. We all know it takes being out there to make those numbers happen. What we **ought** to know is that we need to be out on the streets *all the time!* If a client event isn't going on, find out what's happening in the community and tap into that. It's as simple as checking out the newspapers and calling the Chamber of Commerce.

The key to any successful promotion, whether you're promoting your radio station or client event, is total preparation! Hook your call letters into existing events. Start simple. Get permission to have your station van parked at the entrance of a local ball park. Find out if there's a need for an emcee for an event and offer the professional services of a popular air-personality.

Develop an entire line of logo items: caps, t-shirts, sweats, polo shirts, jackets, handbags, wallets, sun visors, etc., all sold at events to benefit local food banks. Approach event coordinators explaining that items sold don't benefit the station financially; proceeds go to local food banks in the country where the event is being held. The chance for on-air support plus that all-important "warm & fuzzy" created by doing something for the community, opens doors.

Remember, take pictures at the event and include them on your website and include crowds. Thank the sponsor for the opportunity to be involved in their or your event and express the desire to return. Always promote in keeping with the stations sound. If it's not right, **walk-away!**

Top 25 Most Important Promotion Categories

— Banks
— Bars
— Breakfast
— Business
— Car Dealerships
— Charity
— Children
— Christmas
— Cinemas
— Community
— Electrical Stores
— Entertainment Venues
— Events
— Health Clubs
— Hotels
— Jewelers
— Nightclubs
— Restaurants
— Retailers
— Shopping Centers
— Text
— Travel Agents
— Valentine's Day
— Website
— Workplace

CHAPTER THIRTY-THREE
INCREASE RATINGS WITH PROMOTIONS

It's critical that you maximize your listener's engagement with your contest. Incorporate several tactical objectives. The most effective radio promotions, contests & sweepstakes concurrently achieve one or more of your tactical programming goals. These may include:

- Positioning your radio format
- Building your images
- Defining your USP
- Creating free publicity
- Causing brand awareness
- Expanding brand recall
- Setting tune-in appointments
- Increasing listener cume
- Propelling market share

You'll also broaden sponsor revenue, find new advertisers and upgrade non-spot income. Let's take a look at several creative radio promotions from across the country. Even if you don't use these, they might trigger an idea of your own you may implement on your station.

"The Million Dollar Cash Drop"
This is an opportunity to take money giveaways to that next higher level. You allow contestants to skydive landing on a grid of squares—each representing a different amount of money, with one spot (or all spots together), being worth 1 million dollars!

"Free Business Window Advertising"
Your cash spotters roam your market, searching for storefronts featuring signs saying," WXXX Is My Favorite Radio Station!" The spotter awards a $50.00 bill to the person who put up the sign, t-shirts and pens to everyone else at the place of business (i.e. t-shirts and pens to employees and customers alike).

Make sure your contest is exciting for your entire audience. Promotions, contests & sweepstakes should entertain listeners who don't participate.

"The Hidden Mic"
This is a creative variation of "The Secret Sound" but it's actually a hidden microphone. At regular intervals, play audio from that location, providing clues as to where it can be found. You may call a random phone number every hour (choosing from people who have signed up) allowing the first listener with the correct answer to win! Radio promotions like this are perfect for the 'theatre of the mind' medium of radio! They will increase brand awareness, as listeners will ask one another if they know where the mic is hidden. Connect your station brand to your promotion, as "The KC-101 Hidden Mic."

"The Great CD Rush."
Listener has ten seconds (or time limit tied to your actual frequency) to name all the current titles & artists of CDs possible. The listener is awarded all the CDs he/she manages to name within the time limit. This is a great promotion for CHR/Hot AC and Urban radio stations.

Astrology: "What's Your Sign?"
Make this promotion a monthly event, issuing invitations to callers and social media signees who were born under that particular month's sign. Feature an astrologer who will provide personalized horoscopes. You can also use the party to perform some listener research, using a not-too-long questionnaire.

"Beat The Clock"
We hear the ticking sound of a clock, while a cash prize is increasing every second—but the listener participating can be disqualified any second. When the alarm sounds, all the money is one! Because no one can predict when the clock will ring, you have a contest that's exciting for your entire audience. Pre-produce some sound files with both the clock and alarm sounds in them, and let them rotate. Instruct your jocks not to open the sound file upfront, as the wave file would show where the alarm goes off. The DJ will feel the same excitement and surprise as the participant and respond authentically—also to avoid any possible feeling of 'contest fixing.'

"The Fugitive"
This is a more compelling promotion where the listeners will join a 'bounty hunt' for a mysterious person on the run. Throughout the hunt, give listeners cryptic clues concerning where the person is hiding. The first listener who tracks down and actually identifies the runner wins your prize on the fugitive's head. The great benefit is you're moving listeners into physical action and get them on the street to do something.

This allows them to become much more involved with the promotion as well as your station! It can even go viral, as listeners will share clues and answers on social media and their followers.

"Easiest Audience-Recycling Contest Ever"

This contest has been performed by hundreds of stations and works well with recycling your quarter hour maintenance. To win, the caller must know both the question and the answer—both of which have been aired on the station. Give the answer during PM Drive while the question is given during Morning Drive. Both are clearly identified, so it's just a matter of listening to the radio until they're given and then go scrambling for the phone when the DJ asks for the question and answer. Make it worth the listeners while, give them something genuine like a minimum $100.00 cash prize. Have the DJ who gave the money away give it to the listener who won. It's a more personal gesture.

An "Entertainment Guide"

Publish a pocket-sized guide listing phone numbers, addresses and open/closing times for movie theatres, "actual" theatres, any drive-ins still around, concert halls, auditoriums, bowling alleys, skating rinks, sporting parks and arenas, etc. Sell advertising to entertainment and non-entertainment clients, to pay for the printing and provide a profit. Gives the guides away at public appearances, ball parks, books stores, restaurants, etc.

"Free Miles Friday"

Have your station draw from e-mails and social media entries, awarding chauffeur-driven limousines to and from work (or school) every Friday for a month. Broaden the scope of the idea to include secretaries (the limo drives the winner & her co-workers to lunch at some nice restaurant, waits while they eat, then returns them to work). You can also include housewives. The limo driver picks them up at home, drives them to the supermarket while the chauffeur pushes the grocery cart inside the store. Then drives her them home. For maximum effect, use the longest, blackest limousine you can find.

CHAPTER THIRTY-FOUR
PROMOTIONS

The right radio promotions get listeners talking about your brand, and create tune-in occasions that will increase ratings. The following are Win-Win-Win Radio Promotions that are helpful for your station, sponsors, audience and community. I'll cover radio promotion ideas that go beyond the usual

CARS

GIVE ME THE HORN
Have fun with your breakfast show listeners and get them to guess the identity of a car by its horn!

CRACK THE CUBE
Keep your listeners guessing about the identity of a crushed car – perfect for sponsorship by a car dealership.

CHARITY CALANDER
Support your local charity with a special calendar put together by your station.

CHAIN OF FOOLS
Are your listeners fool enough to compete in this totally mad, wacky promotion?

GO TOPLESS THIS SUMMER
Grab your listeners' attention this summer with this fun and exciting car promotion!

HANDS ON A CAR
Give your listeners the chance to win a car simply by keeping their 'Hands On'

LIVE IN IT TO WIN IT
A classic proven winner promotion to give away a car which also increases time spent listening

CASH, CARS AND STARS
A fun contest to play on air and ideal for sponsorship by a car dealership or garage.

MYSTERY VOICE
A classic radio contest proven to increase time spent listening and attracts sponsors.

DIRTY CARS
A fantastic promotion to increase awareness of your station, DJ or sponsor name and have a lot of fun too.

BIRTHDAY KISSES
Your listeners win cash everyday just by knowing their own birthday!

CELEBRITY PHRASE THAT PAYS
A promotion guaranteed to drive your listeners mad trying to guess the celebrities!

CAR-TOONS
A contest to give away a car on air which encourages listening at peak drive times.

£10,000 SAFE
An excellent promotion guaranteed to increase footfall into a client's shopping center or store or showroom.

REVERSE AUCTION
Beat the bid – an auction with a twist, guarantees to get your listeners talking!

BIRTHDAY BALLS
Listeners can win a cash jackpot by listening to either your breakfast show or drive time show and having their birthday ball drawn out on-air.

FACEBUCKS!
A major cross-station promotion tying in your station and website imaginatively capitalizing on the name of Facebook and Starbucks!

CAR SEARCH
A major promotion to give away a new or used car which can be sponsored by a dealership.

WIN A CAR A DAY IN MAY
A major and ambitious station promotion to increase your listening and profile.

RUN TO THE CAR!
Listeners have to run to qualify themselves to win a car – right in front of their own home. a fun and high-profile way to give away a new car with the support of a car dealership sponsor.

WORLD TOUR
A fantastic summer promotion to get your station out and about in your area.

GAME, SET AND MATCH
A fun on-air and off-air promotion focusing on tennis that will generate footfall and create lots of talk ability.

CELEBRITY LAUGHS
A high profile station promotion with benchmark appointments to listen in all primetime shows.

BEHIND THE RASPBERRY
This promotion gives front of mind awareness, appointments to listen and loads of pr and talk ability.

BIRD VERSUS BLOKE
A variation on battle of the sexes – with an extra twist.

HIT IT TO WIN IT
Play the radio version of battleships but with a twist. this interactive promotion is designed to increase listening hours and drive website traffic.

TANKETY TANK
Win petrol in an amusing but simple daily contest for your breakfast show.

WORK YOUR WAY TO THE USA.
A chance for listeners to test their knowledge of the usa and american music both on and off air to win a trip to new york

HOT CARS
a public and community service feature that makes great use of radio and is great for sponsorship by car or security companies

DON'T SAY HELLO
a major station-wide contest designed to raise awareness of your station among non-listeners

THE JOKE'S ON YOU
impress us with your best joke to win a cash prize – a cross-station feel good promotion perfect for sponsorship by almost any business

DIAMOND MINE
a very exciting and attention-getting mobile promotion which can be taken to various sponsor locations.

GUESS THE MILEAGE
a effective car giveaway promotion where the contest's sheer simplicity encourages great listener interest and participation.

THE AUTOGRAPH-MOBILE
a silly promotion which is great fun and perfect for sponsorship by a car dealership.

STAR IN THE CAR
a great interactive contest across your radio station to increase awareness and footfall for car dealerships and shopping centers.

HIT FOR SIX
a fun competition for a car dealership to promote a new registration plate and giveaway fantastic prizes at the same time.

STASH THE CASH
the perfect breakfast show contest to increase footfall at a used or new car dealership.

SERVICE WITH A SMILE
a simple breakfast show feature to image a co-host and give listeners the chance to win prizes for being comedians.

GHOST WASH
a fantastic memorable and imaginative charity promotion in the run-up to halloween.

CAR JACK
a car giveaway contest with a fantastic twist – ideal for sponsorship by car dealerships or showrooms.

CAR PRICE GUIDE
how much is my car worth? your radio station can help in this weekly feature sponsored by a car dealership or showroom.

THE 8.20 SPECIAL
a great way for your station to become involved with a high profile event at a car dealership or showroom.

I WANT TO LICK YOUR FACE
a fun, interactive out-and-about contest for morning shows involving potential embarrassment for contestants

CAR WARS
a 'star wars' branded major station promotion using voting for a lucky listener to win a new car.

WEATHER OR NOT
a fun way to spice up your weather forecasts with listener interaction

DRIVE A CAR, WIN A DIAMOND!
a great contest linking car dealerships and jewelry stores.

CAR HIDE AND SEEK
a fun, interactive treasure hunt style contest to win a car perfect for sponsorship by a car dealership

BABY CRAWL
a fantastic themed promotion aimed at parents which is sure to raise the profile of you and your client by getting newspaper and tv coverage

SIT IN FOR TICKETS
a fantastic promotion involving lots of your listeners trying to win tickets to a concert or sports event

MUMBLING MANAGERS
a fun contest where callers have to identify sports stars or celebrities from a cacophony of voices

BARREL OF LAUGHS
a fun listener-participation event, which promotes a particular sponsor as a community-minded organization, with a family-friendly sense of humor

GOING CRACKERS
a fun christmas contest based around christmas cracker jokes, ideal for a sponsor who wants to be part of the seasonal cheer!

BIRTHDAY BUMPS
a combination of feel-good birthday messages, and a simple, fun, quiz with sound effects and lots of potential for sponsor branding

THE HICKETY HACKETY CHALLENGE
a high-profile highly amusing video contest which involves bars, pubs and workplaces throughout your area

CARWASH KARAOKE
a fantastic sponsorship opportunity for a car dealership whilst creating station awareness

DAMSEL IN DISTRESS
a weekly benchmark idea to help commuters on the way to work, ideal for a car dealer or a transport/driver service

BUSINESS PROMOTION IDEAS

BEST OF YOUR TOWN
establish your station in the local business community through a high profile annual awards event

GET A JOB DAY
help your listeners get started in a new career by creating a new business event.

CHARITY CALENDAR
support your local charity with a special calendar put together by your station.

SUPERSAVER BOOKLET
guarantee advertising spend and get your stations branding through the doors of existing and potential listeners

FEAR OF FLYING
up, up and away! help your listeners conquer their fear of flying through this imaginative promotion

TOWN WEEKS
reach new and existing listeners and businesses through this high profile promotion where

PICNIC IN THE PARK
generate revenue from your clients this summer in a new and interesting way

PUT ME ON THE PAYROLL!
an at-work listening contest that increases time spent listening to your station

TWELVE DAYS OF CHRISTMAS
a tried and tested promotion that never fails to warm your audience and generate revenue for the radio station

BUSINESS BULLSEYE
have loads of fun on-air with this listener interactive competition which targets local businesses.

BUDGET SPECIAL
an informative sponsorship opportunity for a bank, financial institution or the business community.

TRIVIAL PURSUIT
a very interactive promotion that can will increase at work listening and bring out the competitive streak!

MILE OF MEN!
a fantastic valentine's day promotion which generates great pr and brand awareness

ADVICE CENTRE
offer your listeners free advice from experts who are your clients

FIRM FAVOURITES
increase at work listening whilst giving your listeners a treat at the same time

FULL HOUSE
a fun five week promotion based around numbers giving away fantastic prizes that is guaranteed to create talk ability.

WORKPLACE WORK EXPERIENCE!
this promotion will guarantee at work listening and plenty of talk ability and pr opportunities.

FAMILY GOES FREE
make your radio station the hero this half-term by keeping the
kids busy with this flexible promotion

WHO'S MINDING THE SHOP?
a fun interactive contest to build awareness of a client's retail
business and to have listeners constantly thinking of that business.

BEHIND THE RASPBERRY
this promotion gives front of mind awareness, appointments
to listen and loads of pr and talk ability

CLOCK WATCHERS
a new benchmark sponsorship feature generating listener interaction via text and targets workplace listening

FREE FUEL FRIDAY
a big station promotion perfect for attaching a sponsor name
to guarantee footfall for your client.

DREAM JOB
amazing talk ability, pr opportunities, website traffic, interactivity on and off-air, this promotion has it all!

JOB LOVE
a very simple but effective contest perfect for sponsorship by a
restaurant, bar or employment agency.

DESTINATION UNKNOWN
just what you need to run alongside a major sporting event
with listener interaction and sponsorship from bars or nightclubs.

SUPER CASH
an exciting big money cash contest perfect for sponsorship by
a bank or financial business

LIGHTS OUT
an environmentally-aware promotion which has a big impact, creates great pr and can be sponsored by companies wanting to protect their green credentials.

FREE ADVERTISING!
a promotion for local businesses to win themselves a free advertising campaign on your station

WHAT'S COOKING IN YOUR KITCHEN
perfect for sponsorship by a restaurant or food business, this promotion also drives traffic to your website.

WAR OF THE WORKFORCE!
reward your workforce listeners with the chance to win a fantastic day out paintballing

WIN A WEEK OFF WORK
a high profile breakfast show contest for the employees at five companies in your city, town or area

DJS DEN
this fantastic promotion is a radio version of the tv show dragon's den designed to find the entrepreneurs in your audience and attract sponsorship from banks

TEN TIMES
a simple music competition ideal for sponsorship by a retailer celebrating the anniversary of their business

CARER OF THE YEAR
a great opportunity for a business wanting to sponsor a promotion with a 'feel good factor' and which is linked to the local community

DIRTY GREEN MACHINES
a promotion about water conservation and therefore environ-
mentally friendly

BARREL OF LAUGHS
a fun listener-participation event, which promotes a particular
sponsor as a community-minded organization, with a family-friendly sense of humor

RESTAURANT PROMOTIONAL IDEAS

DATE MY DAD
a major promotion guaranteed to get your listeners emotionally involved in a heartwarming story – and earn your station
revenue from a variety of sponsors

CHAIN OF FOOLS
are your listeners fool enough to compete in this totally mad,
wacky promotion?

BIRTHDAY KISSES
your listeners win cash everyday just by knowing their own
birthday!

ELVIS DREAM TICKET
if your target audience is into elvis, they'll love this fun cue to
call contest themed around elvis presley

WIN YOUR BIRTHDAY PARTY
a fantastic birthday prize that will definitely get your existing
listeners talking and introduce new listeners to your station

BIRTHDAY BALLS
listeners can win a cash jackpot by listening to either your
breakfast show or drive time show and having their birthday
ball drawn out on-air.

MILE OF MEN!
a fantastic valentine's day promotion which generates great pr
and brand awareness

DJS CHRISTMAS PARTY
let your listeners eavesdrop on a special event for your DJs

COOL TO SCHOOL
make your listeners' kids the envy of their classmates with this
simple yet effective promotion

BROKEN HEARTS BALL
the ideal event for those unlucky in love on valentine's day

EATING OUT GUIDE
this promotion gives local restaurants and takeaways the opportunity to sell themselves through an interactive promotion
and sponsorship package

THE CHICKEN BONG GAME / FRIEND OR FOE
two friends play a game of 'chicken' to win cash in a twist on
the original bong game.

BEHIND THE RASPBERRY
this promotion gives front of mind awareness, appointments
to listen and loads of pr and talk ability.

BIRD VERSUS BLOKE
a variation on battle of the sexes – with an extra twist.

DREAM ICE CREAM
a great summertime promotion to test the imagination and
ingenuity of your listeners.

TOP TABLES
a great feature to generate awareness for local restaurants

BIG BREAKFAST EXPERIENCE
create a new fun feature in your breakfast show that generates
loads of interactivity

LEANING TOWER OF PIZZA
a fun competition involving a pizza restaurant or takeaway

NOSH OR DOSH
an exciting promotional opportunity for a restaurant with a
moral dilemma…

WHO WANTS TO WIN A MEAL-ON-AIR!
a fun, feel-good contest which plays on the name of the popular tv show.

IF THE SHOE FITS…
a fun promotion for a shoe shop or department store with a
real cinderella ending!

WORK YOUR WAY TO THE USA
a chance for listeners to test their knowledge of the usa and
american music both on and off air to win a trip to new york

SOMEONE SPECIAL
a very simple feel-good contest ideal for retail or restaurant
sponsors and also increasing time spent listening to your station.

PARK FOR FREE
a great feel-good public service promotion for your street crew
to raise awareness for you and a sponsor

THE JOKE'S ON YOU
impress us with your best joke to win a cash prize – a cross-station feel good promotion perfect for sponsorship by almost
any business

JOB LOVE
a very simple but effective contest perfect for sponsorship by a
restaurant, bar or employment agency.

PARLEZ VOUS FRANCAISE?
test your listeners french with this fun valentine's day competition

WANNA LIFT? TAKE OUR LIMO
an aspirational contest to give your listeners a taste of the
highlife supported by a retailer or entertainment business

GET ME TO THE CHURCH ON TIME
who wouldn't want to hear if a bride makes her wedding on
time? a wedding giveaway with a big difference.

CAROLOKE!
a christmas contest capitalizing on the popularity of karaoke
singing supported by a retail sponsor.

DO YOU LOVE ME?
a fun and entertaining breakfast show contest in the run-up to
valentine's day perfect for sponsorship by a restaurant or bar.

FEEL GOOD FRIDAY
your station offers an after-work party to a special workplace
in a promotion supported by a bar or entertainment venue

THE X-MAS FILES
embarrassing and funny stories of workplace christmas events
to win a workplace party from a restaurant or bar client.

HOME OR ROME
a very simple breakfast show contest based around landmarks
in your city, town or area and perfect for sponsorship by an
italian restaurant.

WHAT'S COOKING IN YOUR KITCHEN
perfect for sponsorship by a restaurant or food business, this
promotion also drives traffic to your website.

THE LUNCHTIME LINE
an addictive lunchtime sponsorship opportunity with lots of
listener interaction

NEW YEAR, NEW YOU
celebrate the start of the new year with a new-look you courtesy of a variety of your station's clients.

WOULD YOU LIKE FRIES WITH THAT?
an imaginative, fun contest to raise awareness of items on the
menu of a fast food restaurant or burger joint.

THE BIGGEST DICK IN TOWN
a cheeky on-the-edge contest for a station targeting younger
demographics with a sponsor who wants a cutting edge image

DUELLING DOGGIES
the perfect contest for competitive dog owners which can be
sponsored by a dog shelter or a pet shop.

FATHER'S DAY
a variety of simple promotions and contests for father's day

BARREL OF LAUGHS
a fun listener-participation event, which promotes a particular
sponsor as a community-minded organization, with a family-friendly sense of humor

BIRTHDAY BUMPS
a combination of feel-good birthday messages, and a simple,
fun, quiz with sound effects and lots of potential for sponsor
branding

THE HICKETY HACKETY CHALLENGE
a high-profile highly amusing video contest which involves bars, pubs and workplaces throughout your area

MAN MADE WEDDING
an on-air wedding with a difference – and a total station-wide high profile promotion involving multiple sponsors.

APPROPRIATE BIRTHDAY SONGS
a fun spin on birthday dedications, with a prize for the winning birthday boy / girl

CHAPTER THIRTY-FIVE
MARKETING & SALES DIFFERENCES

People often place sales and marketing together, even to the point that numerous sales jobs are now termed as "Marketing Directors". This combination may seem like it would be beneficial because many managers fail to see a real variation between sales and marketing. Are they correct? How should your radio station(s) view sales and marketing?

Marketing is foundational – practical.
Build a house without a foundation; it holds no substance. Every structure, be it something in the physical world or in the conceptual world needs substance. Remember the 2000s dot com bubble? The problem wasn't that there weren't great ideas; the problem was that the great ideas had no substance. When they were released into the world many ideas simply collapsed because there was no substance. Marketing is the groundwork for a large sales approach. As such, marketing performs several key requirements:

• **Define success**. This may seem strange, success is making sales right? Wrong: success for sales is closing sales. Success for marketing is building your radio stations awareness.

How many times have you talked with someone that would have been a great customer for you only to realize they didn't know you did what they needed? Without marketing, they never will. Word of mouth is great for small companies but only works for growth in severe cases. Defining your success means knowing how many people need to be reached to make a sale. Here is the formula

X Impressions are needed to make Y Contacts to get Z Visits = One Sale

• **Provide consistency**. I once worked with a radio station that had three different messages for the same sales package. Sales used whichever seemed to work, the company promoted on whichever one was the fad of the moment and the radio station eventually bankrupted. Their message was inconsistent; no one really knew what they were about, how they did it or how they could benefit a client.

Marketing "controls" the brand is really saying: marketing manages the same message consistently. Message being the words, colors and designs. And before you get flippant that colors and design don't matter - remember the human brain retains by communicating with several pathways. That is why you remember the words to a song from when you were twelve but have to use your phone for your appointments tomorrow.

• **Explore the possibilities**. The best analogy is marketing goes off in the forest hacking away areas that may or may not lead to something great. Once you've found a place, Sales comes in building a road to see if there is potential for growth followed by Service, which builds the city.

Marketing provides the guidance to know where to go into the forest of business by using educated, foundational analysis and research. This educated approach is why you need professionals, not uneducated people who are loyal but don't know what else to do.

Sales is growth - responsive

Once you establish your marketing, with a nice marketing plan, then Sales moves in to begin dealing responsively with the results of the plan.

• **Cultivate Relationships**. It is a lot easier to fire a faceless corporation then it is to fire Bob who you know so well. Relationship building is the key to growing a diverse product/service offering. A sale is the face of the company. Don't believe me? When was the last time you had a great experience in a retail store? Was it the company or the person you dealt with that made it great? For me, it has always been the person. Anytime someone goes above my expectations, I'll overlook other problems. So will your clients.

• **Provide real-time feedback**. Sales know a lot about what is going on in your market. They can determine where problems are going to be coming to inform management, and marketing. One of the greatest ways is to simply ask them to provide it. When I've sat in Sales team calls that are mostly brow beating sessions by management for not meeting numbers while discounting that Sales is providing essential information about changes in the marketplace; I immediately see the problem that no one wants the real-time feedback being provided. Sales see problems in the short-term, which is why marketing needs that information.

• **Conclude business**. The most important part: putting everything together for a prospect to move to becoming a client. Key to this is realizing a prospect's needs in terms of the solutions offered, that means listening. Taking that information and blending it with the solutions a company offers. Pointing out discomfort before it becomes a problem for a prospect. All these things happen because awareness was created, relationships were built; feedback was acted upon to lead to a strong client relationship.

Marketing comes first, Sales second and Service keeps the client. When the boundaries are set, expectations are established and people can be held responsible for their part in the company. When the lines get blurred, chaos reigns. No client ever likes chaos. Keep marketing and sales separate but working together as a team, allowing them to perform their jobs and empowering success with these straightforward concepts.

CHAPTER THIRTY-SIX
TURN SALES TALENT INTO PERFORMANCE!

Have you ever heard music that was so brilliant, you couldn't even carry on a conversation while listening? I had a friend in college who played like that. Her audiences would be virtually silent as she played, mesmerized by the sound, until her last note when the student body would erupt in vigorous applause!

She practiced both the piano and the guitar often, simply because she loved it, and she often played for the college upon request. I'm not much of a musician myself, and I didn't know a lot about the business then, but those who did were certain that she would be one of the few who actually made a career for herself in the music industry.

But music was not meant to be her calling. Her parents wanted her to go to medical school like both of her brothers had done, and while they appreciated her natural talents, they didn't want her to focus time on them that could be spent studying. Her boyfriend, while also a loyal listener, enjoyed their limited time together and didn't want to share it with an instrument. So, needless to say, she practiced less and less, focused her time on other things, and found herself on a very different path.

This is not a story with a sad ending, but rather, with food for thought. She is now happily married and enjoying both a career in medicine and two young children. She even plays when she can, just for fun, but you can't help but wonder what could have been.

What if her talent had been spotted, encouraged, and consistently developed? What if she had someone who mentored her, showed her the ropes, and celebrated her successes with her? Could she have been the Taylor Swift of our generation? Who knows? The fact is that talent is not sufficient. Whether we are talking about music or talking about sales, talent is key (a total deal-breaker if you don't have it), but it's only the first step in a tricky staircase to climb.

As a radio sales manager, you have the tremendous opportunity to help your talented salespersons' hike what can feel like a mountain and make it to the top.

Here are some ways that you can help them to turn talent into performance:

Dodge the cookie-cutter approach.
Manage each individual in the way that they need to be managed – which will be different than the way the guy sitting next to them needs to be managed. When making your next hire, use a validated talent instrument that measures the intensities of their strengths and weaknesses so you can clearly understand what you are working with. Make sure the assessment you choose is able not only to predict success, but also give you the information you need to build a highly-customized coaching plan that will allow you to maximize their strengths and work around their weaknesses. Build that individualized management plan and refer to it often.

Build a strong relationship.
People work best for a manager who they believe sincerely cares about them. Relationships in the workplace matter! So make sure you take the time to develop those relationships and

show your salespeople that you care about them. Remember important occasions, become familiar with the things they enjoy outside of work, and spend time with them. Most importantly, get their input on what they need from you. Our clients use an instrument we call the Individualized Management Questionnaire which guides them through a list of questions like, "Do you like being given a clear plan to follow, or do you prefer to do your own planning?" Create a list of questions that you can use to uncover how your salespeople want to be recognized, corrected, motivated, and challenged. Anyone can point out their shortcomings, but it takes someone who really cares to show them their strengths and help them to grow.

Don't keep your thoughts to yourself.
Give them plenty of feedback so they can better understand exactly what is working for them and what is not. The best feedback is timely, frequent, consistent, and focused on the big plan so you don't overload them. Make sure you have systems in place to ensure that you are noticing their work because without a specific plan in place, it'll never happen. And remember that the average person needs five pieces of specific positive feedback in order to be open to one piece of corrective (negative) feedback. It's more than worth the effort!

Cheer them on!
Celebrate their successes with them and let them know you believe in them when they fall down and need to get back up again. Encouragement is a wildly powerful tool but a lack of encouragement can leave a gaping hole in the drive of many. Did you know that the number one reason why people leave their jobs is because they don't feel appreciated? If you are celebrating their successes with them, or helping them to consider how they might turn their failure around, your salespeople will know you greatly appreciate them.

Test them.

This does not mean you should put an unbearable burden on their shoulders. No. It means that you should count on them in areas that fall directly in their wheelhouse - so they can be successful and grow in an area where they have talent. Spend time with them as they are learning their way, but don't let them take the easy way out if you know they have the natural ability to push themselves. The fact is that when you spend time developing someone's talent, you can increase performance up to 10 times! There's time well spent.

Talent is rare! We all have many more weaknesses than strengths and there are very few things that any one of us can do to the level of excellence. If you take the time to hire only those who have the kind of innate talent necessary for success, and then you coach them and develop their talent... who knows what they can accomplish! Don't let them get stuck at the bottom of the basement!

CHAPTER THIRTY-SEVEN
EFFECTIVE RADIO SALESPEOPLE

The salesperson's job is to get information from the advertiser in front of the radio listener. Essentially, you're moving information from one source to another. If you're proficient and persistent, you'll make a good living. In this millennium of communication available 24 hours, you have to manage your time effectively and stay informed to your clients wants and needs.

Collect materials regarding your prospects
Get a hold of any trade journals they may subscribe to and read them. Perform a strategy session with your potential new client. This will give you more confidence and allow you to give a better initial presentation. How much time you are willing to invest to make a sale is up to you. If you're proposal is for a $20,000 buy, 15 percent commission is $3,000 dollars. Is it worth doing a few hours' research and writing to place you in a much improved situation to close the sale? Ask yourself a question; is your time worth $1,000 an hour?

Arrange formal written presentations
The time preparing writing presentations should be precisely related to the size of the order you're seeking. Written

presentations compel you to think about your client's problem and make you a better salesperson. Advertising clients appreciate concise, right-to-the-point presentations. It gives them documentation validating their decisions to their business associates in the community.

Conduct face-to-face presentations

Making face-to-face presentations then asking for the order is your job. The reminder of your influence selling activities places you in a position to do the job correctly. The appointment setting, planning, presentation writing and research all places you in the position to ask for the order. If you're servicing a client you already have on the air, make another appointment, assemble more information, arrange another presentation, and upsell the client!

Upselling current advertisers

Remember: The ride down is easier than the ride up! Instead of purchasing a schedule, advertisers are buying name awareness and an action plan that will meet their goals. Most clients on the air are underspending and are frustrated with the radio medium. It's all about frequency. The rest is conversation. If a client needs to spend more (and who doesn't), here's what to do:

Tell the advertising client: "This is the largest schedule you're allowed to purchase on our radio station. Running this schedule will increase frequency, visibility, and you'll be the most important advertiser of the day, week or month you're on the air." Now, hand the client the big schedule with their business name printed on it. Clarify that each name represents one ad and that each individual ad contains an additional five or six impacts.

What happens when the client says, "The schedule is too big." Don't panic! Just agree with the client, saying; "It is a big schedule." Then, hand the client a pen and the schedule and say, "Which of our listeners don't you wish to reach? Just scratch off the commercials you don't desire and I'll re-arrange the schedule."

Now, the client must scratch off his business name instead of: 60s and: 30s. Have any idea how difficult that is? Explore this technique and show the client what running fewer spots means in terms of less name awareness. If the client does scratch off a few names, when he stops, you've closed the sale for all the names and dates that are left! Your client has just committed to purchasing the remaining air dates. Use this tactic to make radio advertising physical and you'll develop more clients and have them close the sale for you.

Dealing with tough objections

If you've sold radio advertising for any length of time, you've heard all of these:

> "Your rates are too high"
> "I don't like the music you play"
> "Nobody listens to radio"
> "I tried radio and it didn't work"
> "My budget is already allocated"
> "I just saw your ratings book and you really slipped"
> "Send me your media kit and call me next week"

Your rates will always be too high. The ratings will constantly be too low. Controlling tough objections requires talented communication skills that get to the **actual** problems. Top billers don't cave at the first sign of an objection. It's usually not the real one in most cases. The best method for handling objections lies in obtaining more information.

Reversing is often the best technique in obtaining feedback. To reverse a client's objection, remain calm. The most successful radio salespeople take objections as well as rejections in stride, treating them as information rather than personal attacks. When reversing, you're demonstrating you've listened to the objection and need more information. When you close the reverse, ask a question that the client must finish. This will "reverse" the objections back to the clients.

Reversing is a great skill for turning a false objection into a real objection. Discovering the real reason a potential client doesn't like your station places you that much closer to the sale. Top performers know objections are just hurdles, not brick walls. Numerous clients will place hurdles up trusting that you'll be the one to leap over them. When you do, you'll be the kind of salesperson they want to have calling on them.

Developing methods for building rapport and sales

Radio salespeople build rapport when they engage the client's jargon rather than their own. Efficient pacing is the skill to acquire. This means copying or mirroring some aspect of the client's behavior. Pace the body language your client is using. Cross your leg at the same time he does. Attempt to mirror the position your client takes. If your client's vocal tone is soft, soften yours. If the client talks slowly and you talk fast, slow your rate of speech down to help build trust.

People tend to like people who are like themselves. This may not always be fair, but it's the truth. If you're talented, you can pace the mood of the client. Pacing gets you and the client on the same even keel. When you are selling easily, this happens naturally. By pacing a client you should be able to establish rapport quickly and with more clients.

Clearly, you don't want to be dragged down by the lousy mood of a client. After you've paced the client's behavior for a while, attempt to **lead.** Settle down with a client for a few minutes. Pace his or her body language. At some point, shift your body language and notice if the client follows your lead. If that happens you've obtained some rapport and the client will be more receptive to your presentation.

Persistent people make their breaks

Radio is fueled by good sales people and is always on the lookout for talented people who can produce. They certainly can come from other sales professions, car sales comes to mind. Any good salesperson can make it in radio sales. Many stations are not opposed to hiring new employees who exhibit a willingness to learn and work hard.

Here's some good news, most radio stations are more than happy to train qualified enterprising people. Like most professions, you'll acquire the lingo over time. The significant skill you'll be taught immediately is understanding Nielsen ratings and the correct manner in which to present ratings to potential clients so they can:

1   Identify who is listening, when, and for how long
2   Understand the demographics your station (s) can provide
3   Why the cost is efficient
4   The type of spot (commercial) inventory is available

Radio stations won't just throw you out into the street and yell "perform." Most will teach you sales skills useful in selling radio time, allow you to accompany a Veteran Account Executive (you're not called Salesman anymore), on client calls, and allow you to become accustomed to the broadcasting universe.

How much you'll make is pretty much up to you. Generally stations will start you off on a salary "draw" until you grow to a point where your sales commissions are providing a higher income than your draw. From there, it's up to you how much money you make. If you're motivated and stick with it, you can do very well.

Whenever you sign a new client offer them a tour of the station so they may see the 'showbiz', after all they're investing in your company so be proud to show off where the magic is located. It's amazing how effective this can be in establishing a long-term association and repeat business. Reward clients and visitors with some 'free stuff' (i.e. branded promotional items, t-shirts, mouse pads, whatever) as this helps create an experience they'll remember.

One last point
Always maintain your rate-card. Don't ever discount! Offer bonuses instead. Once you've started discounting your rate-card, clients will always expect you to do the same, which can really hurt your bottom line long-term. A better approach is maintaining your rate-card but add some incentives such as a small banner on the station website or a pre-determined amount of 'bonus spots'.

CHAPTER THIRTY-EIGHT
COPYWRITING SUGGESTIONS FOR
OUTSTANDING RADIO SPOTS & PROMOS

The most successful radio commercials and promos highlight pictures in words, while touching the audience emotionally. How is this accomplished in 60, 30 or even 15 second's time? You must achieve this by combining creativity and effectiveness.

Choose a core message
Before writing, know what you want to say and why. The best questions to ask yourself are:

• Who is the recipient of this message?
Is it aimed at my entire audience, or a specific demographic?

• What is the main objective of the message?
Is it something new, enlarges recall, or triggers an immediate response?

• What is the significant USP of this message?
Why should your listeners choose this particular company, brand, product or service over another?

Possessing a Unique Selling Proposition is of significant importance. Write a list of each unique aspect that comes to your mind, and pick the one that stands out. A narrow focus will yield big results. You may combine multiple unique aspects into a single one. Make sure every word assists the core message. Let 4 people read your copy, and ask them individually what the single most important item is in your text. Unless all 4 say the same thing you intend to communicate, rewrite the copy and test it with 4 others. Once that works, record your copy, and test that with 4 more people. If required, re-write, re-record and re-test your demo until it's flawless.

As equally important is having a single call to action. Providing listeners too many options creates 'analysis paralysis' and reduces the response considerably. Instead of saying: visit the New Charles Flower Shop on Main Street, call us at 1-800 CHARLES FLOWER SHOP and visit CHARLESFLOWER-SHOP.COM, just choose one thing you want listeners to do immediately. Why not direct them to the website, where they can find all the details on their own.

Incorporate commanding action promoters

Ads for expensive cars are not about expensive cars. They speak to your listeners desire to improve or confirm their self-image. There tends to be a lot of psychology involved in audiences to do what you want. There are 7 action promoters:

• Anger: 'Aren't you terribly frustrated your money market account is worthless? Invest your hard earned money here'

• Exclusivity: 'Show what excellent taste you have by purchasing this exclusive car.'

• Fear: 'Don't do anything to jeopardize your health. Take this, and you'll feel much better.'

• Flattery: You deserve the best and to feel great. Treat yourself with this.'

• Greed: 'Hurry to save 50 percent on our entire stock. Discount ends Saturday.'

• Guilt: 'Don't deny these children what yours have. Donate now.'

• Salvation: 'Do you suffer from heartburn? This will give you relief.'

Include one in your copy, and your spot or promo will become more effective. Combine several action promoters, and the effect will be even greater: "Are you upset with your bankers? They make millions with your money, and you receive 1 cent on the dollar. Turn your back on banks, and invest your money wisely. Our new fund guarantees you a 15% return in just 5 years! But don't miss out. This offer ends Friday. Call us now, 1-800…"

Humor is a wonderful way to add emotion and create rapport. While it easily grabs attention and engages your listeners, humor should always be used to support your main message.

Use a conversational style
Listeners have become highly allergic to almost anything that sounds like a commercial. Make sure your in-house produced commercials and promos don't feel like commercial advertising or hefty self-promotion. Rather than mentioning your brand or solution right away, have a real conversation with your listeners first. Try at all costs to avoid red-flag words like 'sale' and typical clichés that turn your audience off. Focus on listener benefits; not on you and your great product or service. "Don't talk to me about your grass seed, talk with me regarding my lawn," Your audience will ask 'what's in it for me?' and 'why should I listen to this?' Your listener's attention span is at an all-time low. Communicate your benefits right from the start or a creative way, like an opening that draws them in.

Address one person at a time by saying 'you' (instead of we or us), and use the same words your listeners use in everyday conversation. Reach inside the mind of your audience that reflects how they think, so you will trigger silent feedback. If they 'don't wish to be bald,' why not bluntly ask: "Are you afraid of becoming bald?" in a spot that promotes a hair loss treatment. Don't replace 'bald' using fancy words such as 'depilated' or the euphemism 'hairless.' Tell it the way it is.

Tell funny persuasive stories

Engage your listeners with humor or storytelling (or both). Facts tell, stories sell! Humor is a great method to add emotion and create rapport, but never let the humor override the message. Otherwise listeners will share the story with a friend, who will laugh and say: "what was that for?," after which they'll go: "I don't know, but it was funny." You don't actually need humor in your spots or promos. Any compelling story, where people want to hear the end, will work. But having some fun certainly can't hurt and can be a big plus if prepared correctly. Great spots position the core message in between (or right after) the story.

Highlight your pictures with words

Wonderful commercials and promos use storytelling on a higher level. Marketing research shows most listeners will only do something after having imagined it first and radio is the theatre of the mind! Visual copywriting engages your listeners while triggering their imagination, so the subject of the spot (like a product) is in their thoughts as a 'mental picture.' They see themselves driving that Mercedes! As the human brain is wired to fill those gaps between desire and reality, one day there's a good chance they will purchase it. Here are some visual copywriting tips for radio:

• Avoid cliché openings like 'picture this' or 'imagine that' and begin with the story instead.

• Name things people can picture easily. Avoid any abstract words or expressions.

• Use active and present tense verbs in the second person (e.g. 'you can drive this car').

• Place a noun before adjectives; not after (e.g. 'the water is crystal clear and blue').

A commanding part of visualization is to let listeners see the end result of whatever you're selling or promoting. Instead of "WXYZ gives you a chance to win 6 first-row tickets to see Lady Gaga in Rome!," write: " Do you want all your friends to adore you? Listen for a chance to win a trip to Rome for you and 5 friends, where you can get eye to eye with Lady Gaga, standing front row at her Rome concert. WXYZ is making you the star."

Get rid of the waste
It's always impressive to win an award for the best-written commercial. It's much better to turn an advertiser into a life-long client! Write to communicate; not to impress. Your commercials are not a website, so leave out that the company has been there since 1972 and avoid addresses and phone numbers your listeners can't remember. Tell your client to have a site with an easy to recall address (e.g. charliesflowers.com). When you practice 'less is more', the more your 15 second spots will be to the point the better you'll use your 30 or 60 seconds to tell a compelling story which highlights the Unique Selling Proposition. Create your spots to have a strong beginning and end, as listeners will most likely remember those two parts.

Broaden your creative juices

For creative output, you need input. It's that simple. One part is attending movies, concerts and reading magazines making sure you stay in touch with current pop culture and current affairs. Another part is living life: getting married, having children and (hopefully not) getting divorced. It's not difficult to find inspiration if you live a full life and explore many different events. In the movie "Yes Man," actor Jim Carry commits himself for a year to just say 'yes!' to anything the universe is offering him; from Korean courses and guitar lessons to much more.

The advantage of possessing a wealth of skills and knowledge is you can easily associate things, and play the 'what if' game to make new combinations of basically unrelated existing items. What if Jim saves someone's life because he understands Korean and plays guitar? Certainly, this question may have led to that movie scene! Use that same creativity for your radio copywriting.

CHAPTER THIRTY-NINE
THE STATE OF AM RADIO

Here's a well-known fact: NOBODY & I mean NOBODY is dial scanning AM radio. Those days are over! Commercial FMs for the most part, are seen as the most lucrative broadcast entity; further, their owners hope to profit by placing FM signals in cell phones, smartphones and other portable media devices. The FCC acknowledges that many AM licensees are in a struggle for sheer survival.

The once-leading system of broadcasters is fighting to remain viable in the 21st century. When the FCC adopted a rulemaking allowing AM broadcasters to use FM translators, it clearly stated in its report that "the combination of higher-fidelity alternatives to AM radio and increased interference have caused an erosion of the AM audience and loss of younger listeners to other programming means."

According to data from the FCC, there are 4790 AM stations as of December 31st, 2009. There is almost zero growth in the number of AM radio stations from a decade earlier. Until 1978, AM maintained more than half of all hours spent listening to radio, according to the FCC. AM's share of listening hours has dropped to 17 percent, due to difficulties in channel congestion, interference and low-fidelity.

According to data from BIA Financial Network indicates a downward spiral on revenue at AM radio stations. Revenue for commercial AMs in rated markets was nearly $2.9 billion in 2004 although it dropped to $2.4 billion in 2008, the latest figures available. Most of that revenue is generated by the large AM stations in major markets.

AM radio can use every advantage it can get its hands on, just to survive. The FCC allowing FM translators is the very least it can do. Sentiments regarding the future of AM radio in the U.S. It seems as though technical and operating challenges will continue and additional station erosion is very likely. There's a large drop in market value for many AM stations. If the market continues to spiral downward, more licensees will go dark, take down their towers, and sell their land to developers. AM arrays tend to take a lot of real estate.

AM can solve many of its problems with creative programming, being live and local. Create programming not heard on commercial FMs. AM radio doesn't have to be all sports or all talk. Music can be played on AM. Create a "different" format, not heard in your market. As a consultant, I've helped many AM stations get on their feet with creative, original, fresh programming with live 'personalities.' That's a wonderful way to distance you from corporate FMs programmed from far away.

Promote, promote, promote! Get a station van with your logo splashed on either side. Have a part-timer or intern drive the van around town for a couple of hours. Load it with station goodies; pens, coffee cups, sun visors, all with your station logo on them. Have the driver call in several times an hour, stating where their located and how long they'll be there giving out great promotional items. Your station van becomes a rolling billboard. Don't just park it in the station lot!

If it were "my" AM station, I'd be at the opening of an envelope! Develop business relationships by joining your local Chamber of Commerce. Volunteer your best air personality to be at a business grand opening. Personal appearances at restaurants and bars are always a crowd pleaser. This is a great way to become visible in the market without spending any money.

AM radio stations have a unique opportunity to serve their local communities that commercial FMs don't take advantage of. FM radio has, for the most part, become homogenized and nothing more than a "music-box." If you play the same game with satellite or automation all day, you're no better than the FM doing the same thing. If all you're going to do is be a music-box, your listeners can do that much better than you can, without the bad commercial interruptions.

I say 'bad' because most commercials or station promos are really poorly produced. Invest in some good production voices that can crank out those promos and commercials that "stand-out." If you're a listener with an I-Pod loaded with 1,000 songs, you're already your own programmer. Why in the world would you need a radio station, let alone an AM station millennials won't listen too?

AM radio develops a personal connection with its audience, its localism, and its diversity. AM stations have the ability, to become a locally focused radio station. With the lack of red tape and bureaucracy, AM owners are swift to meet the needs of their local community. If insightful enough, AM radio can become the epicenter of everything important in that local community, while still possessing a foothold on independence.

CHAPTER FORTY
YOUTUBE TURNS INTO RADIO'S LATEST TRANSMITTER.

The "Video Killed the Radio Star" line has been hurled at radio countless times over the past four decades. However, radio may get the last laugh. Moving past just on-air audio, one broadcast is showing that a powerful radio brand and a smidgeon of investment can translate well on the new TV enterprise, known as YouTube. So far a single station has logged 100 million video views.

Online video advertising accounted for 8% of total ad spending in 2013, according to eMarketer, and is forecast to hit 14.5% within four years. One radio station benefiting from the trend is Emmis rhythmic CHR "Hot 97" WQHT, New York, whose YouTube channel recently registered its 100 millionth view. But the tendency global hip-hop brand didn't hit the milestone by simply placing a camera in its air studio and repurposing what it broadcasts over the air. "We treat digital as its own separate platform," says Lin Dai, VP of digital programming and entertainment for Hot 97 and its sister video network Loud Digital. "You need to produce and program digital content differently than you do with your radio content."

Dai says its video viewership dramatically took off after it converted an artist green room at Hot 97 into a TV studio. Equipped with TV lighting and a multi-camera set-up regulated by a tri-caster, it allows producers to cut between five camera angles during a single video shoot. The result is a high-quality TV look and feel that Dai says viewers are more likely to consume than interviews shot in a radio studio. The fully equipped TV studio enables the station's digital team to generate more video output sooner. "What used to take 8 hours to edit now takes 1 to 2 hours," Dai says. "We can put out double to triple the amount of content." He says stations looking to succeed in online video need a dedicated digital content team, rather than relying on station staffers who do digital on the side. "It requires a different type of skill sets," Dai says. "You need a team that is passionate about digital that's not doing it part time as a side to a radio job."

The $50,000-$100,000 investment Emmis made to create a TV studio is paying off in web traffic and ad revenue alone. Dai says most of the channel's growth has occurred in the last six months, since the TV studio became fully functional. Hot 97.com gets 1 million unique visitors per month while the station's YouTube channel attracts another 1.6 million monthly views. Astonishing viewership!

The content that Hot 97 streams on YouTube also streams on its own website. The station site caters more to a local New York audience while the YouTube channel's audience tends to be global, with minimal audience repetition between the two assets. The YouTube channel has become so popular that Hot 97 is among a handful of media properties that YouTube allows to sell advertising on its platform through a revenue share arrangement.

Hot 97 has parlayed its digital success into the Loud Digital Multi-Channel Network, an assortment of some 40 websites that is sells advertising for, including sites for rapper 50 Cent and other artists. Crosstown Yucaipa urban AC WBLS (107.5) has joined the network with hopes of increasing views on its own YouTube channel and monetizing them. The most popular content on Hot 97's channel gravitates around the station's iconic personalities like Funkmaster Flex, who hosts a freestyle show with a guest artist, or the station's morning show, which conducts a 20-40 minute interview that can be edited down into a five-minute audio break for broadcast on the station.

"A listener enjoying the interview on their car radio can watch the full interview on their computer when they get to work on our YouTube channel," Dai says. The original web series "97 Seconds," which provides an intimate artist profile, recently kicked off its second season with rapper Macklemore. The clip generated 60,000 views in just three days.

CHAPTER FORTY-ONE
SLOGANS DON'T SELL: PEOPLE DO

You don't sell with slogans.

Advertising is desirability.

Not in a lurid or controlling sense.

One of the definitions of "desire" is "to appeal." Successful radio advertising appeals to the targeted consumer directly in the sales message. But just to illustrate a point, let's fall back on the more common association to the word "appeal."

In this example, "Rob" is a healthy, single adult male who is feeling a bit lonely. He finds himself at a loud, crowded cocktail party where he notices a beautiful, single adult female whom he finds attractive. She has some spirituality about her that Rob finds appealing.

He thinks, "If I had an opportunity to talk to that woman in a quiet, more relaxed surrounding, I bet we'd discover we would have a considerable amount in-common."

In essence, Rob has a sales message that he hopes she will consider acting upon. And he's trying to choose between two diverse expressions of that sales message.

The first is:

"It sure is noisy here. I wish we could talk in a more peaceful environment. There's a wonderful Italian restaurant just up the street with an incredible view of the city. Would you be interested in getting a bite to eat with me while watching the sunset?"

Or Rob could say:

"You've tried the rest, now try the best."

Considering those two approaches, which do you believe has the best chance of succeeding?

It's not bad to have a Positioning Statement that forcefully reiterates your Unique Selling Proposition. Actually, that can be a very good thing.

But a good Positioning Statement — or slogan — can only replicate and reinforce your actual sales message. A slogan without a sales message to back it up is nothing more than Verbal Fast Food.

CHAPTER FORTY-TWO
PORTABLE PEOPLE METER

The Portable People Meter (PPM) is a method to measure how many people are listening to specific radio stations at any given time. It measures not only traditional AM or FM radio stations, but digital broadcasts including HD Radio, Satellite Radio and Internet Radio Stations. The PPM is worn like a smartphone, and detects hidden audio tones within a station's audio stream, logging every time it detects such a stream. Every person who wears a PPM device is called a "panelist" by Nielsen Audio, the American ratings research company who owns PPM.

PPM has been a game changer since its inception in 2007 by Arbitron (Now Nielsen). Top of mind creation is very important in PPM markets. Not for written recall (Diaries), but for today's listener tune-in. You must be the first choice of your audience. PPM research has shown that different dayparts bring a different audience. You must oversimplify how people listen to each quarter hour, and then generate listener events which match the listener's routine.

In both diary and PPM markets, your radio station must possess awareness, and listeners need to know your dial position. PPM data details where people actually tune-in, and how often they return to the station. People who tune in many times during the course of the day are being titled "heavy listeners." Stations that are number one with heavy listeners are known as a base station. The difference between P1 and PPM is founded on opinions (thoughts) vs. facts (actions). P1 shows listener preference: "what is your favorite radio station?" PPM demonstrates listener behavior: "what radio station(s) do you actually listen to?

In a PPM universe, listeners need to turn on your station 'first.' It's up to you not to lose them. In an interesting sideline, even when your audience tunes you out, it doesn't seem to be a problem, as long as they come back often enough. You'll notice a smaller Time Spent Listening (TSL), compromising many different tune in moments. With PPM it's about generating occasions (listener instances) to keep your audience coming back. Cume (referring to the total number of different persons who tune to a radio station during the course of a day-part for at least five minutes) is king in the PPM world. Teasing your audience can be accomplished on-air and off-air through social media outlets such as Twitter & Facebook.

While cume has doubled in PPM measurements, there are techniques that can be used to increase TSL and AQH (Average Quarter Hour). New listeners revealed by PPM show's they are more casual, driving down TSL for individual stations. What you actually find is an increase in average quarter-hour.

There are reasons why individual stations have shown a decrease in TSL with PPM. Casual listeners don't listen to the radio station as often. When their lower TSL is factored in, it reduces overall time spent-listening. PPM measurement also eliminates rounding that occurred in diary entries. Everyone who's ever seen a diary has noticed a pattern where a listener would write down a start time and then draw an arrow through the day. PPM only records when a listener is exposed to the encoded signal.

The PPM reveals listeners listening to more stations. That means individual listener TSL to radio is spread thinner. There's something else broadcasters will have to get used to;

new terms for TSL. The new terms are "Average Time Exposed" (ATE) for daily TSL and "Averaged Weekly Time Exposed" (AWTE) for weekly TSL.

The Portable People Meter solves problems that have plagued diary-based measurement for years. Diaries measure recall, biasing results toward top-of-mind stations. PPM measures actual exposure while capturing instances of listenership that diaries miss. Diaries are filled out by a much smaller percentage of respondents during any given week. PPM measures a complete sample (albeit small) every week. In theory, this should add stability to the results while allowing stations the ability to check ratings for specific one-time events.

Not all broadcasters are sold on the PPM technology. It's been observed that tiny PPM panel changes produce wild fluctuations in ratings, raising questions about the verbosity of the methodology and—unfairly—the effectiveness on an industry that all too often depends upon it.

PPM has taught Radio Programmers three important lesions:

1. Remove damaging content
Damaging or terrible content chases away listeners into the hands of your competitors that are offering a better product. Don't do a bad interview at the wrong time. That's a big tune-out!

2. Teasing is essential
When there's an on-air event transition there's a susceptibility, such as going from music to spots or even song to song. Apart from sound and well-testing content (such as playing favorite songs), teasing is essential to building and not losing your audience. Hold people to the party as long as possible. As a songs ends, say what's coming up. Think who has just joined your audience: use one line resets after a song or break to review and introduce the topic for them.

3. Create listener obsession

Prompt the listeners as to why they tuned-in: highlight your content, such as music, contests, news, benchmarks and personalities. Remind your audience how to use the station: construct a way that will make people listen longer right now ("Your chance to win concert tickets for Elton John coming up in ten minutes"). Encourage listeners to tune in tomorrow or later in the week: creating future tune-in occasions ("Listen tomorrow morning at 7:20 for your next opportunity to win").

Commercial stop sets will 'recycle' your audience. Commercials will in-fact, turn your listeners away. But by the end of the commercial break, a whole new group of users come back waiting for what's next. If you give your listeners a reason to stay, they usually will if there's some specific interesting program content after the ad break.

Train your audience that at the end of the spot break, there's a great feature such as a Music City Minute they won't want to miss. Or some other feature you come up with, depending upon your format. You'll notice a kind of cycling through of listeners. PPM research offers great insight into the audience attention span. The analysis will guide you on how to lessen your commercial breaks during certain quarter hours.

CHAPTER FORTY-THREE
INCREASING LISTENING OCCASIONS AND DAILY CUME

When I looked at PPM surveyed stations in the top 48 markets regardless of format, I found the overwhelming number 1 stations in those markets have a high daily cume as well as an elevated number of listening occasions. It show's getting people to listen more often is more important than listening longer. At least in PPM rated markets. You need more listeners more often to be number 1 and stay there.

I dug a bit deeper and found that weekend numbers were weak and it took a while to increase daily cume again on Monday. After you've shoved your listeners out the door Friday night, it's difficult to get them to return on Monday. My suggestion is to not just become a music box on the weekends, but be as live and local as you can with remotes, personal appearances, contests, phones. Let listeners "get-involved" with your events. You'll be surprised how it will increase your Monday cume.

When observing listening occasions, give your listeners a reason to come back by setting appointment opportunities. This includes daily as well as next-day-listening, (come back tomorrow at this same time.) We have to convert an increasing number of P2, P3, and P4 listeners into P1 listeners by giving reasons on a daily basis. Produce a relationship with these followers through Facebook, Twitter and E-Mail. Make sure your core listeners are reflecting on your radio station, even when they're not listening. Top of mind awareness is key!

It is evident that cume is king in the PPM world. It's crucial that your station becomes consistent and compelling. Consistent refers to the quality of the content, not the actual content. Radio listeners will only invest their time in a station that delivers quality on a consistent basis. Make emotional connections, tell the listener something they don't know and tell it in an interesting story. If you can achieve this, your listeners will become your marketing campaign.

Become the station that stands for SOMETHING and stick with it. Develop your programming into something other than a music box. You're not going to play "More Hits, More Often." More than what, a listener IPod? Nobody believes that to begin with. Its 80's imaging. Pick a position and own it. Whether it's traffic on the 10's, the weather station, the information station, etc. If you don't already have a brand, look around your market and see who and what core audience is being underserved. Then, design your station around your target demo. Over time, this will increase cume to your station.

Many stations and Morning Shows are not using social media correctly. Twitter and Facebook should be used to interact with your listeners, not just tease them. This is a great opportunity to interact with your audience. Remember to update often and reply to responses. Once you respond to a listener's comment you make a valuable connection. That person will share your response with others within their social network. It snowballs from there.

Benefit on major events that happen locally and nationally that your station can own. The Super Bowl, Valentine's Day, The Haiti Earthquake, The Red Cross, local food banks, etc. Event programming requires that it be heavily branded and strengthened during and after. You may need to go commercial-free or if you're lucky to plan far enough in-advance, connect a sponsor with it.

You don't require 10,000 listeners to attend your next station event to be prosperous. The importance is to provide a unique experience that listeners deem worth talking about and otherwise couldn't get on their own. At this point, your station needs to think big and brash. A limited-access, high end party, an invitation only trip, etc.

Become creative on addressing all of these issues and you will be assured of marketing dollars and increased cume. Become strategic and have something to say! Specific appointment tune-ins and strong event programming are crucial to your stations success in PPM.

CHAPTER FORTY-FOUR
YOUR PPM STRATEGY IS OUTDATED:
WORD OF MOUTH MATTERS

It is almost impossible to count the ways in which playing to Nielsen's PPM measurement methodology may provide short term gains for radio ratings, but very much at the expense of the health of radio brands long-term.

It is accepted wisdom that, since PPM supposedly measures *behaviors* rather than *recall* of behaviors, then so-called top-of-mind recall is irrelevant.

After all, why remind folks that you're there when they no longer need to remember what they listened to?

Here's one reason why.

Because top-of-mind leads directly to word-of-mouth and word-of-mouth is the primary factor behind 20 to 50 percent of all purchasing decisions, according to the terrific Jonah Berger book "Contagious: Why Things Catch On."

Berger outlines numerous principles of contagiousness based on extensive research. And one of those principles is called **Triggers: How do we remind people to talk about our products and ideas?**

People often talk about whatever comes to mind, so the more often people think about a product or idea, the more it will be talked about. We need to design products and ideas that are frequently triggered by the environment and create new triggers by linking our products and ideas to prevalent cues in that environment. Top of mind leads to tip of tongue.

This is related to a second principle: **Public: Can people see when others are using our product or engaging in our desired behavior?**

Making things more observable makes them easier to imitate, which makes them more likely to become popular. We need to design products and initiatives that advertise themselves and create behavioral residue that sticks around even after people have bought the product or espoused the idea.

Skewed PPM thinking and the convenient need to shred expense like every asset is a hunk of parmesan cheese has led to a situation where reminding consumers about our brands and making them more public is, more than ever, viewed as a Gift from the Marketing Gods rather than a means of connecting brands with the folks who might desire them on an ongoing basis.

As ever, ironic for a business in the business of marketing.

So PPM-inspired thinking leads us to diminish the importance of top-of-mind and any strategies and tactics designed to encourage it. Meanwhile, by its nature, radio must work extra-hard to be public. You must be the station listeners go to first!

I recall my first visits to Connecticut and New York in the early 80's when almost every car was plastered with bumper stickers for the town's hottest stations. Fans did this to brand themselves in the images of their favorite stations and to publicly display that branding to the world. *They weren't advertising those stations, they were advertising themselves.*

Today, good luck finding cars with radio bumper stickers almost anywhere..

I remember some of the early efforts of stations like 91X

to activate the marketplace with attention-getting promotions like "Show us you're X." These and many other audience-engaging promotions served to make radio brands public and promote top-of-mind and the tip-of-the-tongue it leads to.

I'm not being nostalgic here. I'm making a point about strategy and intention:

Unless your brand specifically seeks out top-of-mind occasions, unless you specifically design ways to make an invisible experience into a public one (as Apple did with those white earbuds), then you may win the PPM battle for a while, but you'll lose the consumer attention war.

CHAPTER FORTY-FIVE
INCREASE YOUR CUME

The New Year is about Radio increasing Time Spent Listening and connecting with your listeners. How well does **your** radio station connect with your listeners?

Always start with on-air contributions. Does your station sound in-the-know, or are you sending your listeners somewhere else for what they want? Constant time-checks and weather remarks in Morning Drive, for example.

Search your capability to increase listeners through your databank. Identifying listener birthdays on Facebook is an immense event. When contest winners receive prizes, make sure there is a personalized note from the air personality who awarded the prize thanking them for listening!

An excellent way to increase cume is by personal contact. Hitting the streets and pressing the flesh. Remember to shake hands, ask their names, and reference a few on your next show. Your role is to reflect the listener's life through your radio station.

It's always much easier to increase new listeners through endorsements from existing audience members!

CHAPTER FORTY-SIX
THE BEST SALESPEOPLE ARE
YOUR AIR PERSONALITIES!

Well coached and developed air talent can be extremely influential when they understand they are *professional persuaders and sellers.* Done properly, they can tie the whole station's package together! Obviously, the various programming and formatics are the building blocks for any radio station. Air talent cements everything together, keeping the building "standing." This is the main reason most jukebox formats fail to deliver long-term results.

People tune to radio for various reasons---music, talk, humor, news, information, or relaxation. It's just that basic. When listeners tune to a station, they must be **sold** on the idea what they are hearing on **your** station is what they want. Music sells a station. Information sells a station. Personalities sell a station through creativity, voice quality, humor, relevant information such as traffic and weather reports, topical discussions, and so on.

The better the information, humor or entertainment, the easier it is to keep listeners tuned to your station (P-1s). Once listeners are **sold** on the idea that your station is one they are searching for, they will be hooked until the time when another station **sells** them a better product.

The best air talent **sells** the station to each potential listener in an emotional manner, one person and one element at a time. It's the Program Director's job to see that every air personality understands how to accomplish this through coaching and air check sessions. Done properly, your station will see **enormous** benefits through better programming and higher ratings and revenue.

CHAPTER FORTY-SEVEN
WHERE IS MY TIME SPENT LISTENING?

TSL continues to be one of the most important listening measurements. Some of the strategies used to improve TSL may seem palpable, but you would be surprised at how many stations don't pay attention to the programming basics. Here are some ideas on how to increase the time your listeners stick around and most important, how many times a day they return to your station.

1. **Spend extra time editing while you reexamine the music log**. Guarantee each 15 minute segment is representative of the heart of the station. Specific areas include:

• Keeping the music tempo on an "even keel". Don't increase the rhythm artificially. A smooth rhythm works well here. Not to slow and boring. Never to intense.

• Place currents where they can be front or back sold by the DJ.

• Avoid bunches of any one group of genres. Example: Too many females, males, country artists etc.

• Check clock rotations to insure that songs are progressing through the day parts and hours properly.

2. **Forget about "forced listening"**. The days of *"Listen all day cause you never know when you can win"* are gone forever. When you're contesting, today's programming strategies include:

Explain exactly when they can win. The goal: get your audience to come back for another listening occurrence. Example:

- "Listen to "Mary" this morning at 10:20 and win $105."
- Tell them what they will win. Generate some interest. E-mail/text your database about it. Sell it on Social Media.

3. **Increasing "occurrences of listening" is the most effective way to increase time spent listening.** The more times a day listeners come to you, the higher the ratings. Here's an example: "Three chances to win today. Listen at 9:20, 1:20, and 3:30." Tip: Avoid using the word "details". It sounds too difficult. Better yet: "We'll explain how easy it is to win."

4. **"Be Outstanding with the Basics"** Whether its diary or PPM, your listeners should always "remember" who they are listening to. Calls always come first & last out of your mouth. Make sure calls are attached to all station elements.

5. **Diary markets are about top of mind recall but this applies to PPM Markets as well.** Listeners ask for call letters, station name, or dial position. Make sure the talent says calls (name) slow and deliberate. Often I hear station names delivered at 1000 MPH. PPM markets, this is still vital for you. The audience must know who you are to create another occurrence. You need to be the first radio station listeners remember to 'tune-in.'

6. **The morning show is always promoting forward.** The greatest bit/content is wasted without effective pre-promotion. Example: "This morning at 7:20, we'll tell you the five worst things you can say to a woman."

• Teases should be carefully worded not to give away the story. Saying "Traffic is next" is not as efficient as saying: "There's a problem on I-75 south at Sunset Road by the Sears store, we'll tell you why next."

• The morning show promo (for next day tune-in) should contain a specific time and reason for a new listening occurrence. Generic will not work. Here's an example: "Join Tom tomorrow at 7:10 when he'll tell you the song to listen for to win $1000.00". Promos that review what they did earlier in the day also do not work. Who wants to hear a rerun of that day's show?

7. No Promotion/Marketing budget? Try email, texting, Facebook, Twitter. Any and all social media. Give your followers an edge in contesting. Use all of the tools you have to "be where your audience hangs out" to produce "another occurrence of listening."

CHAPTER FORTY-EIGHT
EVOLVING TODAY'S AIR PERSONALITIES

Due to present day social media impact, everything has changed for the radio industry. For a handful it represents a threat, while for others it's an opportunity to re-engage with its listeners. When you examine it, it is the most amazing rebirth of our lifetime. We happen to be lucky enough to be here and be a witness of it.

One of the key characteristics of developing any radio station is the air talent you hire and the method you train them in the area of social media. Countless stations are far-off in this area and must pay attention as their listeners are being informed and entertained by other sources too numerous to mention. The internet contains immense influence and power. The opportunities are unceasing.

Each successful radio station is defined by their personalities. Their successful because their compelling to listen to. If you skip a show, you will miss something that your friends will be talking about. And you'll be left-out!

From my experience as a radio programming consultant, good air talents possess these qualities. They are unique, perilous, topical, local and most of all engage their listeners to participate. Today, radio is challenged to find new talents that will keep their appeal high and ratings strong. Radio is not searching for DJ's anymore.

Today's radio is challenging social media content such as Facebook, Twitter and YouTube for TSL. Radio seriously needs to adopt and adapt to the wave of new media smartly and integrate social media into the mix to relate with their listeners or face being left behind and totally irrelevant.

Numerous radio stations have no social media strategy. NOW is the time to get one! For whatever reason, Program Directors haven't thought about how to integrate social media into their programming mix. I've noticed that many on-air talents are using social media without one hint of a plan. How much is too much? How do you go about weaving Twitter and Facebook into your show? What's your exposure and liability? At what point is it a tune out and terminate the mood that your music and show is trying to create?

YouTube has surpassed TV in viewership. Facebook, Twitter and LinkedIn are appealing to consumers on an enormous scale. Radio must lift its game and discover an improved method to be part of the new media landscape or be left in the dust.

Talent Instructions for the New Millennium

Search for air talents that possess a creative curiosity about life and have the ability to discuss it. Urge them to go out and experience the local flavor of the market. Air talents that do nothing more than hang around the radio station all day are normally negated of any real experiences to discuss on-the-air. For God's sake, DON'T hire DJ's. Employ creative people who will inform and entertain with focus and purpose.

Make sure every air talent you work with has a smart phone. No exceptions! It is a tool they cannot afford not to possess. I ask my air talents to use their videos on their smart phones to capture real moments. Then I tell them to practice describing what they saw. This is a great technique to get them to improve their storytelling skills. Ask yourself one question. When you attend a party, who do you hang out with? I'll bet it's with the most interesting and funniest person in the room. The problem with most radio personalities is they have allowed their formatics to get in the way of their creativity.

This is the fault of the Program Director. It's their job to coach talents while developing some new thinking and approaches to their show. Having said that, there are some terrific Program Director's that aid talent to prepare better and much more engaging shows. Outside Facebook, Twitter and LinkedIn there's Tunein Radio which allows you to hear any station in the world via the internet and hear it in real-time.

Program Director's need to meet with their air talent every day to help them focus their show. It's critical that the air talent identify with their audience. For some reason (most likely bad talent coaching), most talents tend to be oblivious to that and miss making the connection with the listener. Make sure the talent is provided with a show prep sheet so they may prepare for their show properly. Many radio syndicators produce and provide prep sheets, some for free.

CHAPTER FORTY-NINE
GET PASSIONATE WITH YOUR LISTENERS

There are enough books on branding to fill an archive warehouse. Some of the finest assistance for radio stations comes to these suggestions that have worked well for Sound Advantage Programming clients:

Establish who you are and where you'd like to be in the marketplace. Associate with the needs, desires and actions of your listeners. Recognize your present brand parity. Is a name change actually required, or just the logo or slogan?

Keep things simple. The more hoops you provide listeners, the more confused they become and less likely to stick-around. If you require explaining your brand, start over!

Become passionate. It's the passionate bond with listeners that wins! Old school radio phrases such as "the hits of yesterday & today" become hollow and don't connect with your listeners. Reflect on the brands in radio that have had staying power. The Big Ape in Jacksonville, Newsradio 88 WCBS New York or the Buzzard WMMS Cleveland.

Dismantle the status quo. Examine your time-tested slogans and be sure your brand method links listeners to your station. Switch your branding and see if it makes sense with your station cluster. If you possess a "New Country" station, does your current country station seem "timeworn" and less appealing?

CHAPTER FIFTY
RADIO LISTENERS EMOTIONAL CONNECTION

It is difficult to find an influence medium which consumers possess a strong emotional bond better than radio. Every listener has a favorite station which they have an emotional connection. Your listeners need to become "Brand Loyal" to **your** station. There's a natural development for radio brands. Consciousness tips to a brand image with the objective of developing a franchise. Numerous radio stations stagger during this step, becoming one of countless stations which play a certain style of music. This makes them just another signal on the radio. Nothing more than music boxes!

Possessing a franchise or (brand) brings you in front of other radio stations in ratings competition. Brands are kings of top-of-mind awareness. But, how do you attain that emotional connection?

Create your station to target a specific audience, and then grow larger as circumstances warrant. This permits concentration on important areas initially.

Build your on-air branding robustly so listeners will not overlook your station. Practice using social media to expand your persona. Social media is relationship constructing a communal experience. Constructing **stationality** is critical! Sell your station's name. Hawk your station brand instead of individual personalities for most stations. Build a brand listeners simply cannot live without.

You must be strikingly diverse and superior to take listeners away from your competitors. Playing more music per hour isn't the solution. Possessing great air personalities, a healthier emotional feeling and extra fun with stronger engagement works like super-glue!

Radio stations that are franchise players, those elements exist. While branding against internet stations like Pandora or XM/Sirius, focus on what makes your station unique. Entertaining air personalities, local weather, time checks, not obtainable from non-terrestrial suppliers.

CHAPTER FIFTY-ONE
IT'S ABOUT CONTENT!

Failures in radio often come because management doesn't take the time to understand the why's of success. The result is a sound-alike radio station in every market. This is what I term homogenization. Originality isn't as popular as it should be, most of the time because radio people don't think they can be original and often being original is merely more difficult than copying. So they slap a new name on some superficial ideas and call it originality.

It's all about content. But it's a bit more than content, unique content, content listeners can't find elsewhere and find entertaining. Maybe it's music stationality, a morning show, an on-air attitude, or all of the above. Spending time on creative development results in your radio station being the original in your market.

CHAPTER FIFTY-TWO
"MAKE IT MEMORABLE"

Have your radio station hold an event, throw a party, start a club or organize a roundtable. At events, make networking part of the fun. Be the station that gets things done, moving and memorable. There's nothing like personal connection, which is why hitting the streets is so vital. Find ways to stay in people's faces. If you create some sense of organization, you can mobilize your listeners into action. Hook your call letters into an existing event. Start simple. Get permission to have your station van parked at the entrance of a local ball park. Hand out those popular and important first impression makers: Bumper stickers! Develop an entire line of logo items: caps, tee-shirts, sweats, polo shirts, car window visors, jackets, handbags, wallets, pens, etc. Find out if there's a need for an emcee for an event and offer the professional services of a popular on-air personality. This may be something organizers failed to include.

CHAPTER FIFTY-THREE
"ATTITUDE"

In my experience as a radio programming consultant/author/talent coach, I've discovered the only common denominator between successful radio stations is **attitude.** The attitude of a radio station is a total composite of the people working there. Good stations have a positive attitude that can be sensed on-the-air. Your listeners may not be able to describe it; they may not even be able to be knowingly conscious of it. But it can be experienced. If the attitude is uplifting, positive and fun, your listeners will return again and again.

Radio takes place in your head. Truly a theatre of the mind experience. You can't smell it, touch it, or see it. An entertainment medium all its own. It exists in the heads of the people who create it. Radio stations with winning attitudes inspire risk taking and learn by setting the example set by management. A good example of effective winning attitudes can be created by a company mission-statement.

Ask the question: "How do we intend to win in our market?" A truly efficient mission statement will balance the possible with the impossible. Give your employees a clear sense of the direction of the company and its goals. People need to feel inspired as if they are part of something big and significant.

Remember to have your staff, air personalities as well as

sales, build a solid mission statement that your company can abide by. People want to do business with individuals they know and have faith in. This applies to advertisers and listeners alike. It's creating a passionate bond your radio station has with listeners that becomes a winning scenario.

All radio stations that possess a driving force from within that sets them apart from the rest will possess a winning attitude. A desire that gives the station or group the fuel to reach their true potential will have positive attitudes. We all know people who exhibit the ability to get along with anyone and everyone. This ability is truly a gift of connecting with others. The capability to build rapport is critical in establishing a winning attitude.

All winning people with positive attitudes develop a strategy as a game plan of life. This road map is something you will use to establish your goals, ambitions and desires. A positive attitude is a strong part of this tactic. Just believing you can earn $50,000 a year is not enough, you must design a plan that gives your life direction and navigates you toward the ultimate achievement, possessing a winning attitude!

CHAPTER FIFTY-FOUR
"INTEGRITY"

My definition of Integrity is doing the right thing, even when no one is watching.

All we can really count on in our lifetime is our integrity. What you do in your professional life tends to bleed over into your personal life. The two tend to be synonymous. When you're thinking about integrity, think about Tiger Woods who, turned out to be the poster boy for absence of integrity. Include Bernie Madoff in this list when his billion-dollar con became known.

You can be the best golfer or broker in the world, but if you lack integrity, that's what people will remember about you. Tiger Woods can mend his golf game; unfortunately his reputation is forever stained. You cannot just get it back. No matter how delicately you forfeit your integrity, it returns to plague you. Somebody untimely finds out and the world will ascertain who you are and what you're about.

If you have not already damaged your personal integrity, here are some steps to attain integrity in your daily life:

Reflect on your interactions with others in the workplace, at home and in social situations to determine specific areas in need of improvement. For example, if you are late for work every day and feel guilty about creating excuses for this behavior, this may be an opportunity to develop greater personal integrity.

Determine your reasons for not behaving with greater personal integrity. For example, you may be pushing unpleasant work tasks on to other employees instead of being honest with your boss about your inability to do the tasks. You may be afraid to admit to yourself or to your boss that you do not possess the right skills or that the job is not the right fit for you.

Face the obstacles that cause you to lie or violate your moral code. This might involve finding a more suitable job, facing your fears about how others may perceive you and/or seeking out counseling to address emotional challenges and insecurities.

Consider all of the relationships at home and work that will benefit from greater truthfulness. For example, if managing a team of employees, be honest and direct with each individual about your expectations and employee performance. Avoid backbiting or gossiping. Refrain from causing harm. Part of developing personal integrity is gauging when and how to deliver the truth. Be careful not to confuse truthfulness with anger-driven and brutally honest confrontation.

Listen to and respect the opinions and decisions of others. Part of possessing personal integrity is acknowledging the human rights of others. Respecting diverse thoughts and decisions is a sign of open-mindedness and integrity. And finally:

Enlist the help of others. Colleagues, relatives and friends who know you well and have your best interest at heart can assist your progress by providing objective feedback on a daily basis about the personal changes you are making.

CHAPTER FIFTY-FIVE
PODCASTING: BIGGER THAN YOU THINK

I predict 2015 will become the year of the Podcast. When talk was king of the hill on radio, live formats did a great job of controlling real-time consumption. The stations and shows were speaking to people sitting for long periods of time. Today, we just don't do that anymore. We're very much in a mobile society. Not just in the method of consuming materials, listeners today expect you to be as portable as you can be.

Ratings on talk radio are tanking faster than the Titanic. How many times a week can you keep hearing the President is doing a bad job, and get a lot of entertainment value from it. Immediate or breaking news is still a huge part of talk radio. When there is a threat, people revert back to their old listening habits. Otherwise; the personalities that were the biggest in talk radio are now demolishing the ratings and revenue of the stations they broadcast on.

This change is due to Millennials—children of baby-boomers. Their media habits are very unique from their parents. They expect you to be where the story is. Millennials want their information bite sized or in small doses. Envision the atmosphere your listeners are in. Walking the dog, on a treadmill, driving to work, having breakfast.

What are people searching for in a Podcast?

- Make it short 20 minutes a day.
- Have intro/outro music.
- Create interviews.
- Have sound cuts of pertinent stories or events.
- Make sure you have commentary.

Require that your show sound and act like a real radio broadcast program. If you have sponsors, the show will sound as if it delivers value. You're placing them on the smartphone where attention is focused. Make certain your show contains a strong brand that listeners wish to hear wherever, whenever they want.

Feature people from your audience on your podcast. When you feature at least one person they tend to embody your entire audience. You'll create a great affection with your listeners doing this. There is nothing as commanding as the sound of the human voice. Your message is part of their lives on a daily basis. You soon turn out to be part of your listener's routine.

Don't place material on your podcast that contains no value to your audience. Your guests and interviews should only be the very best you can get. Don't settle! Be authentic and possess integrity.

CHAPTER FIFTY-SIX
PODCASTING REVENUE STREAMS

If your intention is to increase your income from podcasting, I'll introduce you to some ways to create unique revenue streams while making money podcasting. Create your brand reaching faithful listeners while producing fantastic content that will attract sponsors while generating an income from your advertisers.

Podcasts always cover a specific topic, so it's more than likely your audience contains listeners who possess a great deal of interest in your subject matter. When you combine great content with a loyal following, the prospect for generating advertising dollars will occur. If you can increase the size of your audience and prove you have a specific number of listeners as well as subscribers, then you can contact companies and present a short proposal regarding advertising their companies' products and services on your podcast.

Get some sponsors

Build a genuine relationship with your audience. It won't come overnight, so be persistent. Live your message and the advertising dollars will follow. People hate phonies and can spot them a mile away. Locate companies who wish to be part of your podcast. If you're searching for niche market advertisers, check the concept of your podcast. Are you knowledgeable about the subject matter on the show? Are there any shared subjects that you can endorse? For instance, if you're a mechanic with a car repair show, you could consider finding advertisers from the car parts industry such as Mopar or General Motors.

Concentrate on one area and target local companies before going national. Podcasts also work well which promote a precise geographic region such as Miami Beach. There are plenty of resorts wishing to reach your audience. You're placing your advertisers where the audience is; the smartphone!

You may also wish to offer advertisers commercial recording services, display ads on your website as well as corporate giveaways. It is possible to generate income from your podcast. After you have organized an advancement of your particular podcast, you'll have the instruments to present to possible advertisers. Don't be about your product. If you have a weight loss product as an exclusive advertiser, make your show about weight loss.

Sell your product or services. Take the opportunity to convert loyal listeners into paying customers who wish to acquire your information products or services. If your product is tangible your listeners may just be great customers for you. Another way to increase your bottom-line is to offer some free episodes while listeners pay to access your library to hear the rest. Fusing this with sponsorships will generate a solid revenue stream.

If you have a wonderful interview lined up for your podcast, a sponsor may be interested and sometimes pay for the time. Your audience must fit the sponsors target audience.

Ask for donations

This can be the simplest method to increase your revenue. Have some enjoyment from the experience. Instead of just begging for money, come up with a creative line like, "Do you enjoy the show? Then show me some love and buy me a sandwich!" Or some coffee, or help me pay my electric bill. Something that customizes your show with the listener. I'll grant you, it sounds a little hokey, but hokey sells.

Market an iPhone app with your podcast

One way to make money is to offer your podcast for free but contract out an iPhone application from Wizzard Media, available to any podcaster on a revenue sharing basis. This enables anyone to add value while offering additional content to their podcast. You can add PDF files while moving past shows to her library. This is a wonderful platform to increase listeners and revenue because you're driving them to an apparatus already in use. The iPhone.

CHAPTER FIFTY-SEVEN
THE ART OF BECOMING SUCCESSFUL

Success isn't just about what you achieve during your lifetime. It's about what you *encourage* others to accomplish. Your ability to set objectives and create strategies for their achievement is the **"Principal ability"** of success.

The expansion of this capability and your building it into a lifetime routine will increase additional success and accomplishment in your life more than any other ability. As with most things, you can possess the development of setting objectives by increasing your knowledge and then apply it to everyday life until it becomes involuntary.

Your objective should be to become an unceasing objective setter. You need to develop clear and focused strategies you discover yourself doing each and every day.

PODCASTING RESOURCES

www.radioguestlist.com
www.blogtalkradio.com
www.blogontheradio.com
www.tunein.com
www.broadcasting.live365.com
www.newsgeneration.com/broadcast-resources
www.backtobasicsradio.com/resources
www.resourcesunlimited.com
www.mytalkradioshow.com
www.podcasting-station.com
www.podcasting-tools.com
www.audiographics.com
www.freetalklive.com
www.moneytalknetwork.com
www.naturalsolutionsradio.com
www.specialguests.com
www.speakernetnews.com
www.smalltownmarketing.com
www.rtir.com

Made in the USA
Middletown, DE
19 April 2015